Baseball's Zaniest Stars

Colorful profiles of some of baseball's
wackiest performers. Included here are
the antics of: Casey Stengel, Rabbit
Maranville, Rube Waddell, Bobo Newsom,
Dizzy Dean, Babe Herman, Lefty Gomez,
Germany Schaefer, Satchel Paige and others.

Baseball's Zaniest Stars

by HOWARD LISS

Illustrated with photographs

RANDOM HOUSE
NEW YORK

j 927.96

This title was originally catalogued by the Library of Congress as follows:

Liss, Howard.
   Baseball's zaniest stars. New York, Random House
₁1971₁
   vii, 144 p. illus., ports. 22 cm. (Major league library, 15)

   SUMMARY: Biographical profiles stressing the antics of some of
baseball's more colorful players including Babe Ruth, Casey Stengel,
Germany Schaefer, and others.

   1. Baseball—Biography—Juvenile literature.   ₁1. Baseball—Bi-
ography₁   I. Title.

GV865.A1L56   71–146650
                              796.357'0922 [B] [920]
ISBN 0-394-92142-9 (Library)   MARC

Library of Congress   71 ₁4₁   A C

1704595

Contents

Introduction   vi

1. Casey Stengel   3

2. Rabbit Maranville   18

3. Rube Waddell   35

4. Bobo Newsom   55

5. Dizzy Dean and the Gas House Gang   74

6. Babe Herman   96

7. Lefty Gomez   111

8. A Few More Colorful Players   123

Index   140

Introduction

Back in the 1880's, there was a major league third baseman named Arlie Latham. Like almost every other player in the game, Arlie had his share of troubles with umpires. On one particular occasion he got mad at the arbiters because they refused to call off a game when it was almost dark. Arlie's team was leading, 4-2, and he wanted the victory badly. He realized that almost anything could happen when the light was poor. Yet the umps permitted the game to go on.

Latham told the batboy to get a dozen candles. Then he set them on the bench and lit them. The angry ump came over and blew them out. When the umpire's back was turned, Arlie lit them again. The umpire didn't fool around any more. He forfeited the game to Latham's opponents.

Arlie Latham was one of the first zany ball players, and through the years many others have come along to delight and amuse baseball fans. Some of their antics have been truly hilarious.

For example, Al Schacht—known as "The Clown Prince of Baseball"—once came out on the field wearing a girl's dress with ruffled skirt, and mounted on an elderly sway-backed horse! Schacht also drove an opposing team crazy when he slyly introduced a trick baseball into a game.

Rival batters hit the ball right on the nose, only to see it loop wildly into the hands of the infielders.

Sometimes a man earned a reputation as a zany player when he wasn't trying to be funny. Jim Piersall, who played for the Boston Red Sox and other teams, was considered a prankster for a long time. Unfortunately, Piersall was suffering from nervous tension. He was really mentally ill and wasn't responsible for his actions. Piersall made a great comeback after he licked his illness, and just before he retired, he *did* do some funny things. Near the end of his career, while playing for the New York Mets, he promised that if he hit a home run, he would circle the bases backwards, running to third base, then to second, then first, and finally to home plate. That's just what he did, too!

There have been many zany and entertaining players in baseball. Here are some stories about a few of them.

*Baseball's
Zaniest
Stars*

Casey Stengel, appearing very solemn, poses for a picture in his Brooklyn Dodger uniform in about 1915.

1/Casey Stengel

In 1912 the Montgomery, Alabama, team of the Southern Association had two very interesting players. One was the shortstop, "Kid" Elberfeld. He was a rough and tough old-timer, who had spent many years in the big leagues and was finishing out his career in the minors. The other was an up-and-coming young outfielder who had very little experience in organized baseball. His name was Stengel. He was sometimes called "Dutch," but he had already gotten the nickname "Casey," because he came from "K. C."—Kansas City, Missouri.

Elberfeld took a liking to the newcomer and tried to teach him a few baseball tricks. "When you're on second base and I'm at bat, take a long lead off the bag," Elberfeld advised him. "Everybody knows I like to hit to right field a lot, so chances are the shortstop will play close to second.

"When the pitcher delivers to the plate," Elberfeld continued, "you start for third. The third baseman has to cover the bag, right? That leaves a great big hole between second and third. I'll just tap the ball through the hole and you can score easy."

Stengel thought that was a fine idea and lost no time trying it out. In one doubleheader he had a great day at bat, getting six hits in eight trips to the plate. Early in the first game Casey was on second when Elberfeld took his turn at bat. Casey was anxious to start moving toward third.

But the young player had one bad habit. He was so interested in the base he intended to steal that he forgot to watch where the ball was hit. He concentrated on getting a good lead and taking off for third as soon as he heard the ball hit the bat.

Three times he followed Elberfeld's plan. The pitch was delivered to the plate and Stengel took off. But each time Elberfeld hit a line drive which was caught. Each time the ball was thrown to second and Casey, who was nearing third, was doubled up easily.

The third time this happened, Stengel had rounded third and was heading for home. But the enraged Elberfeld was running up the third base line toward him, brandishing his bat, ready to clout the rookie on the head. As the crowd roared with glee, Elberfeld chased Stengel back around the bases. Casey escaped a cracked head only because a few teammates held Elberfeld back until he cooled off.

A big league scout named Mike Kayhoe watched the game, and later he was asked what he thought of Casey. "Stengel is a good hitter," replied Kayhoe thoughtfully. "Also, he has a good arm, he fields well and he's fast on his feet. But there's still something wrong."

"What's that?"

"Well," said the scout, "Stengel is a real good player—from the neck down!"

Charles Dillon Stengel was born in Kansas City, Missouri, on July 30, 1890. As a youngster he learned a lot about baseball—including a few tricks—from his older brother, Grant. When Casey was about twelve years old and Grant was fourteen, they worked out a sneaky play.

Casey was pitching and Grant was at shortstop. Hidden in Grant's pocket was a nice round potato. A runner reached second base on a hit and Grant took the relay throw from the outfield. He rubbed up the old ball, but instead of tossing it back to Casey, Grant hid it in his glove. He did throw something to his brother—but it was the potato.

Grant went back to his position. When the runner on second took a lead, Grant sneaked over and tagged him with the hidden ball. The other team began to howl and soon a free-for-all started. The Stengel brothers had to run all the way home, chased by the other team.

Casey started his professional baseball career by getting a tryout with the Kansas City Blues. He said he was a pitcher. The first time he took the mound, the batters began driving the ball out of the park and against the fences. Casey got the message. He said he was really an outfielder.

But that wasn't quite true either. In fact Casey had played the infield in school. But he was left-handed and it is almost impossible for a left-handed thrower to play second, short or third. He could get away with it in school, but not as a professional. Casey had never played much outfield because whenever he went back for a long fly ball, he usually tripped over his own feet. Still, he could hit, and the Blues thought that perhaps he might learn to play the outfield someday. Stengel was farmed out to Kankakee, Illinois, of the Northern Association.

At Kankakee, Casey was at least enthusiastic. Before practice he would go out to the field, which was across the river from a mental hospital, and a player named Scheetz would hit long fly balls to him so that he could practice going back for the ball. He would make the catch and throw the ball back. Then, not wanting to waste any time while the hitter got ready again, Casey would drop his glove, back up a few yards and practice sliding, using the glove as a base.

One day a teammate watched Stengel shag flies and then suddenly slide at his glove on the outfield grass. He turned to a friend and said, "Stengel won't be here next year."

"You mean he'll go up to the big leagues?" asked the friend.

"Naw. I think he'll be over there," he said, pointing to the mental hospital.

Casey didn't stay with Kankakee long, not because he was promoted, but because the whole league folded up. He was shifted to Shelbyville, Kentucky, in the Blue Grass League. Then the Shelbyville team disbanded and Casey was sent to

Maysville. And when the season ended there, he went back to the Kansas City Blues for a couple of games. Thus Casey Stengel spent his first professional year with four teams in three different leagues.

In 1912 he played for Montgomery and then for the Brooklyn Dodgers, beginning his long, colorful major league career. The Dodgers were already gaining a reputation as a zany team.

During spring training in 1915 the players were discussing a strange stunt that had been pulled by Gabby Street, a fine old-time catcher. On a bet, he had caught a baseball which was dropped off the top of the Washington Monument. One of the Dodgers wondered if it would be possible to catch a baseball dropped from an airplane. The players decided to try it.

A girl pilot named Ruth Law was hired to fly over the ballpark in an ancient plane that was built only a few years after the Wright Brothers' first flight. A fellow named Kelly, who was a trainer with the Brooklyn club, agreed to ride along and drop the ball while the plane was over the playing field.

When the plane came over, there were a number of players on the field. They saw a round object come sailing out of the plane, and they began to circle around under it, as though it were a super-high pop fly.

Among the "fielders" was Dodger manager Wilbert Robinson, who was having as much fun as any of the players. Finally he called, "I got it! I got it!" The other players backed off to let him make the catch. Just then the wind came up and the object, which was falling at terrific speed, began to sail away. Uncle Robbie misjudged it slightly. The object bounced off his glove and smacked hard against his chest. It broke open and splattered juice and pulp all over the amazed manager. For some reason Kelly had dropped a grapefruit instead of a baseball!

Casey added his own odd sense of humor to the Dodgers. One year in spring training, he was playing in the outfield. As he trotted to his position, he noticed a manhole cover not far from where he normally stationed himself. He pried up the cover and saw that the hole was about four feet deep. Down in the hole was a faucet. Evidently this hole was used to store a rubber hose for watering the playing field.

So Casey crouched down into the hole and pulled the cover over his head. If anyone saw him disappear, they didn't complain. He peered out over the edge like a soldier in a foxhole, waiting for a ball to be hit his way. Then a batter hit a high lazy fly. Casey leaped out of the hole, dropped the cover, went back and made the catch.

Still, Casey could take the game seriously, at least once in a while. In 1916 when the Dodgers were fighting for the pennant, he came to bat against Grover Alexander, one of baseball's all-time great pitchers. Alexander was tough enough in an ordinary game, but in a tight contest he could really fire the ball.

With the score tied at 1-1, Casey was trying hard to get on base. On an inside pitch Casey swung hard and hit the ball with the handle of his bat. It sailed high in the air and with the help of a wind whipping out toward right field, it just cleared the fence, making it a home run. Home runs were rare in those days. Any man who could hit ten in a year was a hero. Casey was so delighted with his lucky homer that he stopped at each base and brushed it off with his cap.

Stengel finally had a dispute with the Dodgers about his salary for the following year, and in 1918 he was traded to the Pittsburgh Pirates. One day during that season, when Casey and the Pirates were playing in Brooklyn, the famous incident of the bird took place.

One of Casey's old buddies with the Dodgers was a pitcher named Leon Cadore. Cadore was very fast with his hands. He could do card tricks and roll a coin around his fingers just like a magician. He was out in the bull pen when a sparrow swooped down near him. With a quick swipe of his hand Cadore caught the bird. Stengel, who was in the outfield, saw what Cadore had done. On his way to the dugout at the end of the inning he stopped to talk with Cadore.

"Give it to me," said Stengel.

"What are you going to do with it?" asked Cadore.

Casey just winked. Cadore gave him the sparrow and Casey stuck it under his cap.

When Casey went to bat that inning, the Brooklyn fans welcomed him loudly. Those who liked him cheered. There were also some loud boos. Casey treated them all the same. He dropped his bat, bowed low and raised his cap. Of course the sparrow fluttered a moment and then flew off.

As the crowd gasped in disbelief, Uncle Robbie, Casey's former manager, shrugged and turned to the player sitting next to him.

"I always knew that Stengel had birds in his top story," he said.

Robbie was hardly in a position to criticize. His own top story was a little odd. Once before a game Robbie gave his Dodgers a long lecture about being alert. He threatened to fine any player ten dollars if he committed a bonehead play. When he finished his speech, Robbie went to the plate to give the umpire his starting lineup. But instead of handing him the roster, he gave the ump a laundry ticket by mistake.

Casey spent three seasons with Pittsburgh and most of two years with the Philadelphia Phillies. In 1921 he found himself playing with the New York Giants under their stern, ill-tempered manager, John McGraw.

McGraw took no nonsense from anyone, as Casey learned to his regret. The Giants manager warned all of his players that if he caught them drinking, it would mean a stiff fine. One day Casey visited a barber shop and got a shave, a haircut and a large dose of bay rum, a popular rum-scented after-shave lotion. He walked into the clubhouse smelling like a distillery.

Playing for McGraw's New York Giants in the first game of the 1923 World Series, Stengel slides into home with the winning run in the ninth. He hit an inside-the-park home run.

"Stengel, you know my rule about drinking!" roared McGraw. "That'll cost you $100!"

"B-but . . ." sputtered Casey.

But McGraw only grew angrier. "For talking back, make that $200!"

"You've got it all wrong," Casey tried again, but McGraw wasn't listening.

"Now it's $300! Got anything more to say?"

Casey shut his mouth. It was the most expensive hour he ever spent in a barber's chair.

Casey could also help McGraw sometimes. One day the field was quite muddy after a rain, and McGraw wanted the game called off. Umpire Bill Klem thought it should be played.

But Casey had an idea. During the pre-game

warmup he trotted out to the base paths and began to slide heavily into first, second and third bases. Again and again he launched himself into the bags, tearing up the muddy base paths.

"What do you think you're doing?" Klem demanded.

"I'm practicing my sliding. No rule against that, is there?" asked Stengel. "Players can take batting practice and fielding practice, so why can't I take sliding practice?"

"You're ruining the base paths," Klem said, pointing to the furrows.

"That's not *my* problem," shrugged Casey. And as McGraw smiled broadly, Klem was forced to call off the game.

Casey Stengel's playing career came to an end in 1925 after thirteen years in the big leagues. He managed in the minors for a while, and in 1932 he became a Brooklyn coach under manager Max Carey. When Carey was fired in 1934, Casey took command.

As a manager, Stengel soon learned that fans could be as crazy as ballplayers. Brooklyn was languishing in sixth place and showed no sign of going any higher. In one game the Dodgers were four runs behind, but in the middle of the game the team rallied to load the bases. With the pitcher due up next, Casey called upon his spare catcher, Gordon "Blimp" Phelps, to pinch-hit. Phelps wasn't much of a fielder, but he was big and could hit the ball out of sight.

Phelps came through with a towering drive

into the bleachers, and the grand slam homer tied the score. But Brooklyn fell behind again, and in the ninth inning they were trailing by four runs again. The team rallied once more to load the bases. But by then Casey had used up all his pinch hitters. As he was pondering his next move, a loud-voiced fan called out, "Stengel, you dope! If you hadn't used Phelps before, you could use him now!"

Casey's Dodgers were not always easy to handle. One afternoon they were playing the Phillies in Philadelphia's Baker Field, which was so small it was called the "Bandbox." The right field fence was a very inviting target because it was so close. And it was made of tin. When a ball hit the fence, the whole park rattled with a loud BOOM! The Phillies usually tried to take advantage of the nearby tin fence by using a lot of left-handed batters who could pull the ball to right field.

On this afternoon "Boom Boom" Beck was pitching for the Dodgers. He was hardly a great pitcher, losing almost twice as many games as he won. The Philadelphia batters were enjoying Beck's pitching immensely. But the Dodger rightfielder Hack Wilson wasn't. Wilson was a great hitter but he didn't enjoy his fielding chores and today the line drives were bouncing off the tin fence one after another. Wilson had been chasing baseballs until his tongue was hanging out.

Finally Casey had had enough. He strolled out to the mound. "You've had it," he told his pitcher. "Gimme the ball."

Stengel (far right) talks with his 1936 Dodger team.

"No, Casey, I'll improve. Let me stay in," pleaded Beck. But Casey insisted.

Angry at himself, angry at the Philly hitters and angry at Stengel, Beck turned and fired the ball out to right field. It hit the fence on the fly with another loud BOOM.

Wilson may have been too tired to pay attention to the game or perhaps he was daydreaming. But he suddenly awoke to hear the loud BOOM caused by Beck's throw. Thinking it was another hit, he chased madly after the ball, picked it up and fired it into second base as the crowd laughingly applauded the marvelous bit of "fielding."

After managing Brooklyn, Casey performed the same duties for the Boston Braves. The results were no better. As he told reporters, "There are two types of ball players, professionals and ribbon clerks. The professionals can execute the plays. The ribbon clerks should be in some other kind of business. On this ballclub I've got a lot of ribbon clerks." He left Boston in 1943.

In 1949 the New York Yankees announced that their new manager would be Casey Stengel. Up to this point Stengel had compiled a fair record as a player and a long string of losing seasons as a manager. Yankee fans, who were used to having the most powerful teams in baseball, were amazed that Stengel had gotten the job. They thought of him as a clown. But Casey was a surprise.

From 1949 through 1960, a total of twelve seasons, he won ten American League pennants and seven World Series. He had tremendous players, like Joe DiMaggio, Mickey Mantle and Whitey Ford, but he also proved that he was a shrewd manager.

With the Yankees Casey also gained another reputation—as the originator of a new language. He seemed to talk non-stop, skipping from one topic to another, and almost always leaving his listeners completely confused. Arthur Daley of the New York *Times* called Stengel's brand of talk "Stengelese" and often quoted Stengel in print.

A typical statement by Casey went like this, "I can bat Andy Carey here and drop that feller to eighth, which I don't wanna do so that it don't discourage him none. And if I put the other feller in right except that Noren's goin' good and that's why I'm stuck." Daley claimed he understood

After winning the 1949 World Series, Stengel (front center) and the Yankees celebrate. The championship was the first of many for the team.

Casey and sometimes "translated" his talk into English.

The Yankees fired Casey after the 1960 season. The Yankee fans, who had made fun of Stengel in 1949, were angry that he was let go and Casey wasn't happy about it either. Still, he was 70 years old and it seemed time for any normal man to retire.

But Casey was not a normal man. Once again he surprised everyone and returned in 1962 to become the first manager of the New York Mets. In a way, managing the Mets was like returning to his earlier days in baseball. The Mets were a new team started with the left-overs of other teams in the majors, and they were a worse team than the ones Casey had managed in Brooklyn and Boston —mostly ribbon clerks. Casey called them his "Amazin' Mets."

In 1967 Casey broke his hip and was forced to retire for good, 55 years after he first played in the major leagues. But in 1969 when the Mets surprised baseball by winning the pennant and the World Series, Casey came back to join in the celebration. Most fans agreed that if anything in baseball was more amazing than the Mets, it was Casey Stengel himself.

2/Rabbit Maranville

In the past the 5-foot, 5-inch ball player had been nicknamed "Stumpy" and "Bunty." Then one day a little girl saw the slender, mischievous-looking young man bouncing up and down, and she called out, "You jump around just like a rabbit." Soon everyone knew him as "Rabbit" Maranville.

Rabbit, who first reached the major leagues in 1912, was an imp. An opponent might get angry at him, but he couldn't stay angry long. Rabbit's argument with Jim Thorpe was a good example.

Jim Thorpe was a fantastic athlete. He had won two gold medals in the 1912 Olympics; he could box, he could wrestle; he played both professional baseball and football. In short, he was a formidable opponent.

One day Thorpe, who played for the New York Giants, steamed into second base on an attempted steal. Maranville, who was playing shortstop for the Boston Braves, planted his foot in front of the base so that Thorpe couldn't touch the bag with his foot. Thorpe was called out.

"You little shrimp, you blocked me!" said Thorpe, angrily dusting off his pants.

Young Rabbit Maranville in his early days with Boston.

"What about it?" snarled Rabbit. "Go back to the dugout, you big ape, before I punch you in the mouth!"

"Why, you sawed-off peanut—I'll kill you for that!" yelled Thorpe, advancing menacingly.

Rabbit retreated a few yards. "Oh, yeah?" he shot back. "And you're just the guy who can do it!"

It took a couple of seconds for Thorpe to understand Rabbit's retort. When he did catch on to the joke, the big man grinned, shook his head and trotted off the field. How could he stay mad at that? It was impossible.

And because Rabbit Maranville looked so helpless, nobody could believe that he would dare get into a fight. Rabbit knew that, and on at least one occasion he took advantage of it.

Boston second baseman Johnny Evers had just tagged out big Heinie Zimmerman, a hulking brute of a man. No doubt Evers had made the tag harder than necessary, for Zimmerman leaped up and rushed at Evers. Immediately, the players of both teams rushed out on the field and began swinging at each other. While Zimmerman was still trying to reach Evers, Rabbit sneaked around him and punched Heinie on the side of the neck, knocking him down. Heinie got up with a roar of rage and started back into the fight. Rabbit saw that the big guy would never be satisfied until he had hit somebody. So Rabbit decided to risk his own neck.

"Take it easy, Heinie," Rabbit said, pulling

Zimmerman out of the scrap. "I'm the one who hit you."

"You? Rabbit, you're such a little shrimp you couldn't hurt a mosquito," said Zimmerman. "I know, it was Moose Whaling, or Butch Schmidt."

"No, honest, it was me," said Rabbit earnestly.

Zimmerman smiled. "You're a great guy, Rabbit," he said. "I know you're just trying to take the blame for someone else. Okay, I'll stop fighting." And the two men walked off the field arm-in-arm.

If Walter James Vincent Maranville had listened to his father, he would have been a steamfitter, not a baseball player. He was born in Springfield, Massachusetts, on November 11, 1891. In those days ball players were looked upon as a rowdy bunch who were too lazy to earn a decent living. Rabbit's father was a policeman, and he didn't think much of baseball or those who played the game.

But Rabbit loved to play, and when he was offered the magnificent sum of $750 to sign up with the New Bedford team, he jumped at the chance. Of course the New Bedford manager, Tommy Dowd, had a few tricks up his sleeve. After he gave Rabbit the money, he talked him into buying an insurance policy that cost $323. It so happened that one of Dowd's relatives was an insurance agent and he needed the business.

By 1912 Rabbit was with the Boston Braves in the National League. He played in only twenty-six games and hit a weak .209, but the way he

fielded was marvelous to behold. In the mind of
George Stallings, the Boston manager, this was
the way the position should be played. And the
manager liked the kid's spirit. He wasn't afraid to
talk back.

Rabbit had realized that he had to win the job
of shortstop from a player named Artie Blues,
who was Stallings' nephew. Maranville didn't beat
around the bush. He went to Stallings and said,
"How about it, do I have to beat out your whole
family?" Of course Blues was hardly any competi-
tion. There was only one other shortstop in baseball who could field as well as Maranville, and
that was the greatest of them all, Honus Wagner.

Maranville became one of the finest umpire-
needlers in history. There was no malice in the
way he heckled them; he was merely having fun,
and they were all targets for his practical jokes.

One day umpire Bill Finneran was having a
tough afternoon in Brooklyn. He couldn't seem to
satisfy anyone—both teams were shouting insults
and so were the fans. Finally, Rabbit came out of
the dugout and handed Finneran a pair of binocu-
lars.

"You'll see pretty good now," said Rabbit,
walking away.

Another time Philadelphia shortstop Art
Fletcher and umpire Bob Hart came to blows.
Fletcher landed a punch on Hart's face and was
tossed out of the game. This was too good an op-
portunity for Rabbit to miss. He came up to the
umpire and looked solicitously at his face.

"Why Bob, you're bleeding!" cried Rabbit in mock horror, pointing to a small cut near his nose. "Let me help you."

Rabbit took a small bottle of iodine out of his pocket and dabbed it on the cut in a long streak which started near Hart's eye and ended up below his nose.

Then Rabbit "found" another cut and streaked iodine on that too. Soon he discovered another cut, and then another. Originally Hart had one tiny cut near the nose, no longer than a scrap of fingernail. But Rabbit, the great doctor, "found" three or four more cuts and kept putting iodine on them. Soon Hart had orange iodine streaks covering his face completely! Fortunately for Rabbit, Hart didn't find out about it until after the game.

Rabbit always found some new way to amuse himself and his friends. For example he once waded into a pond outside a St. Louis hotel and caught a goldfish. Some bystanders swore he ate the goldfish.

When Rabbit heard the story he denied it. "I didn't eat that fish," he said, "I just bit it." He also kept pigeons in his hotel room. And he often traveled with a parrot on one shoulder and a monkey on the other.

On another occasion he suddenly jumped into the Charles River fully clothed and swam across. Why? He just didn't feel like walking across the bridge. For Rabbit that was as good an excuse as any.

Maranville takes a fielding pose for the camera. His glove seems small and badly shaped by modern standards.

In spite of their liking for Rabbit, his teammates also knew that he could be a pest. One day in a hotel a few of them decided to have a friendly game of cards.

"What about Maranville?" asked one of them. "You know what happens if he gets into a game. Or even if he stands around and watches."

"Yes," sighed another. "He'll get into our hair. We've got to keep him away."

So the players sneaked down the hall and locked Rabbit in his room. Then they went to another room on the same floor and began their poker game. Suddenly they heard a tapping on the windowpane. There was Rabbit, grinning and making faces through the glass. He had crawled along a ledge, twelve stories above the ground from his own window to theirs.

That was not the only time he scared his friends either. He once challenged a teammate named Jack Scott to a wrestling match. It was obvious to everyone that Rabbit couldn't win even if Scott wrestled with one hand tied behind his back.

But Rabbit had a plan. Just before the match started, he put some soap chips into his mouth and took a mouthful of water, which, of course, he didn't swallow. Scott grabbed Rabbit in a hold and began to twist his neck. Then the nutty Rabbit opened his lips and began to foam at the mouth. For a second or two Scott thought he was wrestling someone who had rabies, and he let go with a yelp of horror.

Rabbit was a clown and a devil. But he was also a remarkable baseball player, the kind who would do anything to help his club win a game.

In 1914 the Boston Braves were dead last in the National League standings in the middle of July. Then they began an amazing drive to the pennant. One of the important cogs in the Boston machine was Rabbit Maranville. He fielded like a demon, and while his average was a lowly .246 that year, many of his base hits were timely. They kept a rally going or drove in important runs.

On at least one occasion he won a game by using his head. The score was 0-0 in the bottom of the ninth, the Braves had the bases loaded with two out, and Maranville came to the plate.

The opposing pitcher slipped in two strikes and Rabbit was desperate. He crouched and leaned over the plate so that his head was in the strike

Rabbit with a mischievous smile and a baggy uniform.

zone. The pitcher, thinking that Rabbit would jump back, sent a curve ball winging in toward Rabbit's head. But the tough little shortstop didn't back away or duck. He stood there and let the ball hit him on the head!

The baseball rules forbid anyone to get in the way of a pitched ball on purpose. But umpire Charlie Moran admired the courage of the little jokester. He is reported to have said, "I'll allow it —provided Maranville can walk to first base." The opposing team was furious, but Rabbit managed to walk to first and forced in the winning run.

Many years later baseball fans were amazed at Willie Mays' famous "basket catch." Mays would draw a bead on the ball, then hold his hands down around his belt buckle and make the catch. Rabbit Maranville was doing the same thing forty years earlier, but he called it "The Vest Pocket Catch."

Rabbit would camp under a high popup, tap his mitt a few times, then make the catch with his hands held smack against his stomach. Other players tried to imitate him, but they often got hit on the head by the baseball or missed it altogether.

Later Rabbit did a vaudeville act with the vest pocket catch. A stagehand would throw the ball high, all over the stage, while Rabbit would go after it, making fancy catches. But he quit the act in disgust when the stagehand got tired of throwing pop flies one night and threw a few line drives at Rabbit. The audience thought it was funny, but Maranville almost had his head taken off by one such throw.

Nine years after he had come up with the Boston Braves, Rabbit Maranville suddenly learned that he had been traded. Neither his popularity nor his playing ability had declined, but the offer was just too good for the Braves to turn down.

After playing for twenty-one years, Pittsburgh's magnificent Honus Wagner had retired. The Pirates were desperate for a new infielder to take his place. In three years they had found no one who could plug up the shortstop hole.

In 1920 Pittsburgh gave up three players—two outfielders and an infielder—and $15,000 in cash for Maranville. The Braves were in financial trouble, and no doubt the money was as important as any of the players.

Rabbit was welcomed in Pittsburgh with open arms, for there were several players there as zany as he. Among the cutups were second baseman Jim "Cotton" Tierney, pitcher Chief Moses Yellowhorse, who was a full-blooded Pawnee Indian, and Charlie Grimm, a left-handed banjo player on his off hours who also was a better-than-average first baseman. If fans wanted a little fun at ballgames, they got it in Pittsburgh.

In one game the pitcher suddenly stopped pitching. After the game had been delayed a few moments, Grimm, Tierney and Rabbit gathered around at the mound.

"What's wrong?" asked one of the infielders.

"I want a drink," replied the pitcher. And he meant *whisky!*

"Here? In front of all the fans? Are you nuts?" demanded Rabbit.

"We're playing a ballgame," reminded Cotton Tierney.

"If I don't get a drink right now, I won't pitch," said the hurler stubbornly.

It happened that one of the three infielders had a pint flask of whisky in his hip pocket. The trio of fielders gathered around in a tight circle, the pitcher's head suddenly disappeared from view, and a few seconds later popped up again. The game was resumed.

After the side was retired, manager George Gibson asked Rabbit what the conference was all about.

"Oh, nothing," replied Rabbit airily. "The pitcher's athletic supporter was binding, and he didn't know what to do in front of all these people. We just helped him out, that's all."

Maranville showed his versatility in 1924. A young man named Glen Wright had came up to Pittsburgh. Wright was a steady hitter and a great fielder at shortstop. Rabbit was shifted to second base, where he set a major league record by handling 933 chances in one season.

After the 1924 season Pittsburgh owner Barney Dreyfuss made a deal with the Chicago Cubs. He gave them Grimm, Maranville and a pitcher named Wilbur Cooper in exchange for three Cubs.

"I've decided," said Dreyfuss, "that it was time

we got rid of our banjo players."

And then came another bombshell in the life of Walter Maranville. On July 7th, 1925, he was appointed manager of the Chicago Cubs. Rabbit lasted only two weeks. It just didn't seem right to the management to have a manager who wandered through a train throwing buckets of ice water at his players. He seemed less grown-up than the rest of the team.

Rabbit showed up next with the zany Brooklyn Dodgers. But he didn't last there either. Before the end of 1926 he was sent down to the International League.

But he returned the following season, this time to the St. Louis Cardinals. In 1928 he helped lead them to the National League pennant. There was still plenty of life left in the old boy!

Rabbit was back with the Boston Braves again in 1929 and finished out his career at his old stamping grounds. He did a little coaching, played shortstop and second base, and continued to be his old lively self.

The Braves were a terrible team in those years. A couple of seasons they were last in the league and didn't rise higher than fourth place throughout the whole decade of the 1930s. Fortunately Rabbit was on hand to provide some laughs for the few paying customers.

Once, in 1931, when the Braves were playing the St. Louis Cardinals, Boston was losing, 12-0, and most of the fans were hardly paying attention to what was going on. Rabbit soon got their atten-

Maranville, now 43 years old, tries to make a comeback after breaking his leg in 1934.

tion. He called time out and called in the whole team for a conference in the infield. The nine players went into a football-type huddle, broke out of it, then lined up in a football formation. Rabbit called signals, the baseball was snapped back to him, and then the players ran around tackling and blocking each other. It was a few minutes before the amazed umpires could break up the horseplay.

Even when he was over forty years old Rabbit could still do a good job in the infield. In 1930 he led all shortstops in fielding with a .965 average. In 1932 he led all second basemen in fielding with an average of .976. It seemed that he could go on playing forever. The fans loved him, and the infield was one of the few bright spots of the Boston team.

He went through the 1934 exhibition season in fine style. In the final pre-season game, against Brooklyn, disaster struck.

He had already hit a homer off Dodger pitcher Russ Van Atta, and later he got on base again. Rabbit was on third when he got the signal to steal home. Rabbit took off in full stride and tried to slide around the catcher, who was legally blocking the plate, waiting for the throw. Rabbit's leg got tangled up in the slide, and when the dust had cleared, he was lying on the ground grimacing with pain.

It was the fourth time in his career that Maranville had broken his leg, and at his age he knew he'd never be the same again. Although he did try to come back in 1935, the old steam was gone. He played only 23 games. And then he hung up his spikes.

The Boston fans held a "Rabbit Maranville Day" in September of 1934. Some 22,000 people sat in a dreary rain to honor this happy-go-lucky performer. In fact that was one of the largest crowds of the season for the Braves.

Everyone who had ever watched Rabbit Maranville play baseball fell in love with the puckish, always-grinning, peppery little infielder. Even the Japanese, who consider baseball their own national pastime, tried to copy his vest-pocket catch. Maranville had visited Japan in 1931, and the fans there made him a hero.

A tribute to Rabbit's fame and popularity came from one of America's great humorists, Will Rogers. Hearing of his broken leg, Rogers wrote, "When Rabbit Maranville breaks his leg at the opening of the season, that constitutes America's greatest crisis."

Rube Waddell.

3/Rube Waddell

Connie Mack, the manager of the Philadelphia Athletics, strode into the locker room and looked around anxiously. Most of the players were already in uniform, getting ready for the game which was to start in two hours.

"Where's Waddell?" he asked one of the coaches.

"Don't know, Mr. Mack," was the reply. "He hasn't come in yet."

"He knows he's supposed to pitch today," snapped Mack. Then he sighed, as if he knew Waddell would disappear sooner or later. "Some of you start looking for him."

The coaches did not have to be told where to find Rube Waddell, for they already had a pretty good idea. They poked into a few taverns, and sure enough they found the missing pitcher. He was happily tending bar in a saloon.

It wasn't the first time Waddell had forgotten to show up at the ball park, and it wouldn't be the last time either. On some days Rube just seemed happier somewhere else. He liked to stand behind a bar and pour drinks for people and have one himself. If the sun was shining and there was a mild breeze, Waddell might just take the day off and go fishing. Or chase a fire engine. Or join a parade. Or get into a sandlot baseball game with a group of youngsters.

George Edward Waddell was a happy-go-lucky clown, a tall, strong man with the heart of a little boy. His antics caused his managers and coaches many sleepless nights and worried days. But nearly everyone liked Rube. He was good-natured and generous—and he was one of the best left-handers ever to pitch in the major leagues.

Waddell was born on October 13, 1876, on a farm just outside the village of Butler, Pennsylvania. Even before he was a teen-ager, he was plowing his father's fields behind two mules. This hard work turned the muscles in his arms into bands of steel. Once in a while he would stop work to throw stones at the crows which were stealing the seeds out of the ground. Later on he used to boast that he could knock down a crow on the wing— and do it throwing lefthanded or righthanded.

During the lazy summer days young Waddell also found time to play baseball with the village team. Most of the players were much older, but he was a better pitcher than anyone else for miles around, and he kept getting better with every game. After a while other village teams wouldn't play against Butler if Waddell was pitching—he was just too good. Big league scouts began hearing rumors about the teen-ager who was striking out almost every man he faced.

Waddell didn't sign with a baseball team, however. One day a minstrel show came to Butler, and when Rube saw the parade, he knew right then and there that this was the life for him. He asked for a job, got it and ran away from home.

Some months later the minstrel troupe stopped in DuBois, Pennsylvania, to put on a show. Leading the parade was a boy in a colorful uniform and a furry shako hat, expertly twirling a baton. It was Rube Waddell. Baseball was temporarily forgotten; he was having the time of his life.

But this was to be the day of his return to the diamond. That same afternoon a ballgame had been scheduled between the DuBois village team and a team from the town of Punxsutawney. A number of fans had come with the team from Punxsutawney eager to place a few bets on their team. But nobody in DuBois would accept, because their team didn't have a single good pitcher. However, a man named Henry Spuhler, who managed the local hotel, had recognized Waddell in the parade. He had seen him pitch a few times, and Spuhler realized he had a chance to win a lot of money. He sought out Waddell and took him aside for a private talk.

"Young man," he said, "how would you like to earn ten dollars this afternoon?"

"What do I have to do?" asked Waddell.

"Pitch for DuBois against Punxsutawney."

Rube thought it over. "Nope," he finally decided. "I've given up pitching. I'm a minstrel man now."

But Spuhler would not be put off. "I'll make it twenty dollars."

That was a lot of money in those days. Rube scratched his head thoughtfully and replied, "Tell you what, mister. I'll pitch for twenty dollars. But only if you let me wear the same clothes I wore in the parade."

And so, wearing his red tunic and big shako hat, Rube Waddell pitched a shutout for DuBois, striking out nineteen batters. When the minstrel show left town that night, Waddell stayed behind. For he was the new hero in town, and the fans insisted that he keep on pitching for them.

Waddell pitched around the small towns of Pennsylvania for a time and finally made up his mind to see if he was worthy of the big league. Back in 1897 Louisville was one of the teams in the National League. One day the tall, gawky young man walked into the team's office. He was wearing a dinky little cap, country-cut clothes and carried a cheap straw suitcase.

A Louisville fan noticed him on the street and saw right away that he was no city boy. "Hey, look at the rube!" he shouted. Hearing that, Waddell turned, grinned and bowed from the waist. He didn't take offense. In fact he thought it was funny. And the name stuck.

The records show that Rube didn't stay with Louisville very long that year. He lost one game. There were two reasons why he was farmed out. First, although his fast ball was great, he was only twenty years old and too inexperienced to stick in the big league. Second, the Louisville manager began to realize that Waddell was the most undependable baseball player in the United States.

One night a fire broke out in an old wooden church near the team's hotel. The players rushed over to help put out the fire, and Rube gladly joined them. After the fire was out, Rube was trudging wearily back to the hotel when he saw something glistening in the road. It was a diamond brooch! The next morning there was an ad in the newspaper offering a reward for the brooch. Rube returned it to the owner, collected the money and disappeared. He was missing for days, and when he did show up at the clubhouse, manager Clarke decided that this crazy young man needed some minor league experience before he could be trusted in the majors.

Rube was farmed out to Detroit of the Western League. But he didn't stay there very long either. The Detroit manager fined him fifty dollars for some offense, and Rube didn't think it was fair. He just packed his bag and left.

When Rube Waddell became a great star, many fans claimed they "discovered" him. A typical argument might have gone like this, "I saw him pitch up in Canada," one might say. "I knew right away that he'd be one of the best some day."

"How can that be?" another fan would interrupt. "Only a couple of years ago I watched him play out on the west coast."

A third fan would remark, "You're both crazy. Not too long ago I saw a minor league game in Grand Rapids, and there was Rube Waddell, big as life."

Strangely enough, all three fans would be right. After he jumped the Detroit club, Waddell wandered up into Canada, where he pitched semi-pro ball. From there he went back to the minors in the United States. No matter where he pitched, Rube's fast ball and curve moved down enemy batters. Very few minor league pitching records were kept in those days. However, one player who was with Waddell in Grand Rapids said, "That year Rube won about thirty games and hardly lost any. When he felt like pitching, nobody could touch him."

Rube turned up with Louisville again in 1899, and he won seven games while losing only two. Perhaps, if he had settled down right then, he might have become a major league star much earlier, in spite of all the comical things he did. But Rube just didn't want to work hard. He liked to have his fun.

The following year Waddell didn't show up in Louisville. Instead, he played briefly for Milwaukee, which had just joined the new American League. After that he played a few games with Pittsburgh in the National League and then headed west to end the season pitching in the Pacific Coast League.

It is quite likely that Rube got tired of traveling around the country, because he spent the 1901 season pitching for the Chicago Cubs. He won fourteen and lost seventeen, and while that wasn't a particularly good record, even his teammates admitted that they kicked away a few victories with errors and failure to hit at the right time. Even though he stayed with Chicago, Rube still took a few days off whenever he felt like it. He was told time after time that he had to act like a major leaguer, that he was too old to play with kids or to go fishing whenever he felt like it. But Rube didn't listen. Finally the Cubs let him go, and Rube settled in Punxsutawney near his old home town.

Connie Mack, the manager of the Philadelphia Athletics, realized that Waddell had the makings of a great pitcher. Perhaps, he thought, other managers didn't know how to handle Rube. Probably they were too impatient with him. Mack was

Connie Mack, manager of the Philadelphia Athletics, in about 1905. He managed the Athletics until 1950.

a kindly, soft-spoken man. Maybe he could succeed where the others had failed. He went to Punxsutawney and had a talk with Waddell. In 1902 Rube was with the Athletics. And he proceeded to beat the ears off the rest of the American League!

During spring training Rube pulled one of the wildest stunts in the history of major league baseball. It happened down south, where the Athletics were playing an exhibition game on Easter Sunday. The fans called Rube all sorts of names, but he didn't seem to mind, for he was used to minor league fans. Then someone threw an egg at Rube. It hit him on top of the head and dripped down his face.

That was one of the few times Rube Waddell was angry. Slowly he wiped the egg from his face. Then he turned to his grim teammates. He called in all the outfielders; then he told the second baseman, third baseman and shortstop to sit down. Only the catcher and first baseman were in playing position.

Then Rube turned his attention to the batters. And he struck out the side with a dozen pitches, using only his blazing fast ball!

For the next six years Rube Waddell was among the top pitchers in the majors. He won more than 20 games four seasons in a row, and altogether he won 131 games while losing only 72.

The year 1904 was especially outstanding for Rube. He won 25 games and he struck out a total of 343 batters. That record stood until 1946 when it was finally broken by Bob Feller of the Cleveland Indians, who fanned 348 batters. Also in 1904 Rube struck out sixteen batters in one game against St. Louis, and it took many years before that record was broken.

That season Rube Waddell was the talk of the American League. Whenever the newspapers advertised that he would be pitching, huge crowds turned out. Players on other teams tried to figure out ways to make Waddell lose ball games. One pitcher on the St. Louis Browns got a good idea: if Waddell was tired *before* a game, he couldn't pitch very well. So he started an argument with Rube.

"Think you're so good? I'll bet you five dollars I can throw a ball farther than you can."

"It's a bet!" responded Rube. "How can we prove it?"

"Just come out to the ball park before the game."

Rube showed up and both pitchers trudged out to deepest center field. The idea was that each pitcher would throw a baseball toward home plate and see which throw went farthest.

The Brownie pitcher faked a hard throw, but it only went as far as second base. Then Rube wound up and let the ball fly. It zoomed across the field and bounced about ten feet in front of the plate.

The Brownie pitcher pretended to be astonished. "Let's see you do that again," he demanded.

So Rube threw again, and again, and again. He made about fifty throws, each one bouncing on or near the plate. The St. Louis pitcher pretended to be convinced and handed over the five dollars. Rube's arm, he thought, was now absolutely dead.

That afternoon Waddell struck out fourteen batters and breezed to an easy victory. As he was walking to the clubhouse, he spied the disconsolate St. Louis pitcher.

"Hey," he called out, "thanks for the workout this morning. That was swell practice."

Such great pitching made Connie Mack glad he had hired Waddell. But Rube never changed his ways. Once, in the middle of a ball game, he suddenly stopped pitching, raced out to center field and jumped over the fence. He had heard a fire engine going by, and he wanted to see what was burning.

Another time he failed to show up for three days. The coaches looked all over Philadelphia. He wasn't in a tavern and he wasn't chasing fire trucks. Finally he appeared—leading a parade up Main Street, wearing a huge shako hat and twirling a baton.

On still another occasion, when he was scheduled to pitch, Rube suddenly appeared on the field only ten minutes before the game. He raced toward the clubhouse, pulling off his shirt as he ran and shouting that he was ready to go. Later, after he had pitched and won, the exasperated Connie Mack asked where he had been.

"I'm sorry, Mr. Mack," Rube apologized.

"Y'see, I was umpirin' this game between some twelve-year-olds, and I kinda forgot what time it was."

Rube was always doing things that puzzled his teammates and coaches. Once he was caught pouring ice water on his left arm before a game.

"Are you nuts?" screamed the coach. "You're supposed to warm up your arm, not cool it off!"

"I've got to do this, coach," Rube explained mildly. "Y'see, I've got so much speed in my pitchin' arm, if I don't slow myself down, I'll burn off the catcher's mitt with my fast ball."

With a typical country boy's way of thinking, Rube never could understand why anyone needed more than one suit of clothes at a time. When his suit got very dirty, he asked the front office to advance him some money so that he could buy a new one. He bought the suit and was about to throw the old one away when a teammate, who was about the same size, stopped him.

"Why are you doing that, Rube? That suit is still good."

"It's dirty," Rube said, pointing out the many stains.

"Can't you have it cleaned?" asked the teammate. Rube shrugged. "Don't throw it away, give it to me. I'm sure it'll fit."

Rube gave the suit to his teammate. Later his new suit got dirty. So he swapped again, giving up the dirty new one in exchange for the old one which had been cleaned and looked quite good.

Rube was so trusting that his teammates were

Rube Waddell as a St. Louis Browns pitcher in 1907.

constantly playing tricks on him. Rube would find life-like toy snakes in his pocket. Or he'd open an innocent-looking package, only to have a jack-in-the-box fly up into his face. Rube would laugh harder than those who played the joke on him.

Only rarely did Rube get angry, and when he did, he usually went off by himself in a corner to brood about the way he was being wronged. Sometimes he became very annoyed with his batterymate, Ossie Schreckengost. They were roommates, and in those days most hotels provided one double bed in a room instead of two single beds. Schreckengost had one bad habit which drove Rube to distraction: he ate crackers in bed. When Rube complained, the catcher would grin cheerfully and offer his pal a couple of crackers. Rube complained to Connie Mack, but the manager shrugged and said there was nothing he could do about it.

One night Rube had an idea. A short time later, Mack heard a tapping on his door.

"I'm in bed, but come on in," called Mack.

Waddell walked in. He took a sandwich out of his pocket, filled with limburger cheese and onions, and crushed it on the sheets of Mack's bed. "I brought you something to eat in bed, Mr. Mack!" Rube roared. "Now see how you like it!"

Later Rube refused to sign a Philadelphia contract unless there was a clause which prohibited Schreckengost from eating crackers in bed. Sheepishly, Schreckengost agreed.

But Rube's fellow ball players found other ways to fool around with him. Once Waddell and a few buddies were taking a ride on a ferry when one of them suddenly yelled, "Woman overboard!"

"Where? Where?" cried Rube, rushing anxiously to the rail.

"Down there! Don't you see her? Save the woman, Rube. I can't swim."

Obligingly Rube leaped into the water and began to hunt for the drowning woman as his teammates on the boat roared with glee. Of course nobody had fallen overboard. It just seemed like a good time to have some fun with Rube, and his friends took advantage of it.

Yet they knew that if someone had been in danger, Rube would have risked his life without a second thought, hoping only to be of service. During the winter of 1905 Rube happened to be in Lynn, Massachusetts, when a store caught fire after an oil stove was accidentally upset. Rube was just passing by the store when he saw the smoke and flames. He rushed inside, picked up the stove, carried it out and threw it into a snowbank. Only his heavy overcoat and gloves saved him from serious burns.

Another time, while he was duck hunting, he saw a nearby rowboat suddenly overturn, and a man was flung into the water. By the way the man was floundering, Rube knew immediately that he couldn't swim. The weather was cold, the wind was whipping up the water, but Rube didn't hesitate. He rowed out to the man, dove in and brought him safely to shore.

Once a teammate named Danny Hoffman was hit on the head by a pitched ball. An ambulance was called, but it didn't come quickly enough. Rube knew that Hoffman might die if help didn't come soon. So he slung the beaned batter over his shoulder, ran off the field and into the street, commandeered a passing carriage and took Hoffman to the hospital. There he helped nurse his friend, holding ice packs to his head and staying at his bedside all through the night.

Rube Waddell could handle enemy batters, but he never did know how to get along with women. He was married a couple of times, but things never worked out with his wives. First of all, he was too carefree to bother about coming home some nights. And on a number of occasions he got mad and threw things at his mother-in-law. Rube was in and out of jail because of his wives. Several times when he was walking down the street with a friend, he would suddenly duck into a doorway and hide. Then he would explain that he'd seen one of his former wives across the street, and he had not paid her the support money to which she was entitled.

In order to earn extra money during the winter months, Rube took all sorts of strange jobs. He would pose as a mechanical robot in a store window, or wrestle alligators for two dollars a match. One winter he agreed to act in a play, titled "The Stain of Guilt." His role called for him to save a girl and beat up the villain. Rube acted his part so enthusiastically that several villains quit in disgust, because they were tired of getting beat up so convincingly. Rube himself finally had enough of acting, and one day he walked out of the show and didn't come back. The next anyone heard of him, he was a bartender in New Jersey.

Rube pitched for the Athletics until 1908, when he found himself with the St. Louis Browns. He was getting older and was just starting to lose the hop of his fast ball. Still, his first year with the Browns wasn't bad at all. He won 19 and lost 14.

The Browns wanted to keep Rube out of trouble during the off-season, and someone came up with a marvelous idea. Since he liked to hunt and fish so much, why not give him a "job" hunting for the St. Louis team? So Rube was given a weekly salary and told to hunt ducks or deer and bring them to the Browns' office. Once a week he would show up with some game. He was paid just enough to last for a week, and always in one-dollar bills. Everybody was happy. Rube got his paycheck and had a chance to go hunting all the time; the St. Louis officials took home pheasant, quail, duck, venison, rabbit and other delicacies for their tables.

All good things must come to an end, and soon Rube's career in the majors was over. In 1909 he won eleven and lost fourteen. In 1910 his record was three wins and one defeat. Rube was finished and he knew it. But he still felt that he could pitch in the minor leagues for a while. Maybe his fast ball was gone, but surely his great experience was worth something.

Rube joined Minneapolis of the American Association and stayed with them for three years. He worked as a "spot pitcher" and helped them win three pennants. One season he helped his team in a way that only Rube Waddell could devise.

Minneapolis was engaged in a tough pennant race, and a crucial series was coming up against the Toledo Mud Hens.

"We've got to figure out a way to handle that guy Yingling," said the Minneapolis manager. "He's Toledo's best pitcher. If we can get around him somehow, we can take the series and keep our lead."

"Leave Yingling to me, skipper," said Waddell. "He won't bother us."

The next day Rube didn't show up at the ball park. Neither did Yingling, the Toledo pitcher. Both hurlers were gone the following day and the day after that as well. Minneapolis didn't miss Rube too much, because his great arm was just about dead. But the Toledo manager was frantically trying to locate his missing star pitcher.

Four days later, after the series, Waddell strolled into the locker room carrying a huge string of fish. "Where have you been?" roared the Minneapolis manager.

"Taking care of Yingling like I promised. He didn't pitch against us, did he? Here, skipper," he added, "have some nice fish. I can't use 'em."

Rube continued his explanation. "I took Yingling out to Lake Minnetonka for some fishing. It was so nice out there, and we had such good luck, we decided to stay as long as the fish were biting. That Yingling sure loves to fish."

Since Minneapolis had won the series against Toledo, Rube's manager decided to say nothing more. But then the team got a whopping bill from a fish market for Rube's fish. Rube and Yingling hadn't been to the lake after all. Where had they gone? To this day nobody knows!

Waddell poses with a bat for the photographer.

In the spring of 1912 Rube happened to be in Hickman, Kentucky, when a flash flood struck the community. He pitched in and helped, standing in cold water up to his knees, lifting sandbags, trying to keep the flood from spreading. By the time the rampaging waters had receded, Rube had a bad cold. He never did recover fully.

Rube Waddell pitched for the last time in 1913, in the Northern League. By then he had no fast ball and no curve, but he tried to get by on cunning and courage. Even the minor leaguers beat him; he won only three and lost nine. Rube looked weak, he coughed almost continuously, and sometimes he had trouble getting out of bed. The next year he was dead at the age of thirty-seven.

Perhaps it was fitting that Rube Waddell died on April 1st—April Fools Day. He had been a genial clown all his life, giving pleasure and thrills to friends and fans. But he had died broke and alone. There was only a simple cross to mark his grave. However, not everybody forgot about him. When Connie Mack heard what had happened, he collected some money from a few of Rube's friends, added a bit of his own cash and had a respectable tombstone placed over Rube's grave. Rube was also remembered by baseball when he was elected in 1946 to the Hall of Fame for his great feats as a pitcher. But he is best remembered by his fans—as the craziest and most entertaining player of his time.

Bobo Newsom fires a pitch for the Washington Senators.

4/Bobo Newsom

It was the opening day of the 1936 baseball season. The President of the United States, Franklin Delano Roosevelt, grasped the baseball with a smile and held it up as if to throw, smiling at the great crowd. A dozen photographers knelt down in front of his box seat, snapping pictures. He wound up and tossed the ball to a group of baseball players. Then the game between the New York Yankees and the Washington Senators began.

Neither team scored in the first two innings. In the third inning Yankee outfielder Ben Chapman tapped a short, twisting bunt along the third base line and raced toward first. Washington third baseman Ossie Bluege raced in to field the ball.

On the mound for the Senators was a barrel-chested, right-handed pitcher named Bobo Newsom. He stood near the mound, hands on hips, as Bluege moved toward the ball, his body bent over, hands reaching for the skidding baseball. Bluege knew that Chapman was one of the fastest men in the game, and in order to get him at first, he'd have to throw in a hurry. He picked up the ball with his bare hand and fired toward first with a sidearm motion.

Normally, when a pitcher sees such a play coming up, he ducks low so that the ball won't hit him. Maybe Newsom was thinking about something else, or perhaps he was admiring the way Bluege was making the play. Bluege's throw zipped across the diamond and smacked into Newsom's jaw with a crunching thud.

The pitcher's head shot backward. As the ball bounced wildly across the infield, he held his head, then waved his arms and staggered around the mound like a wounded eagle, roaring with pain. His body shook from side to side; he stomped and he kicked and he wobbled.

Time out was called. The Washington manager and the entire infield gathered around their star pitcher.

"How are you feeling, Bobo?" asked Bluege anxiously.

"Wow! What a sock!" winced Newsom.

"Listen, Bobo," said the manager, "I'll call an ambulance and we'll get you to the hospital . . ."

"Forget it!" said the pitcher. "The President of the United States came here 'specially to see ol' Bobo pitch, and that's just what I'm gonna do!"

So Bobo Newsom went back to the mound, took a warmup pitch or two to make sure he could still see the plate and then proceeded to pitch a 1-0 shutout over the Yankees!

Newsom's jaw was broken in two places. Later the manager was asked about the accident. "Oh, Bobo's all right I guess," he said. "The doctors fixed him up. He just won't be talking so much for a while," he added with a twinkle in his eye.

Having a baseball hit him on the head was nothing special in Bobo Newsom's career. On another occasion a batter hit a hard line drive right back through the box. Newsom couldn't get out of the way in time. The ball hit him just over the forehead and bounced all the way into center field. Once again Bobo refused to be taken out. He finished the game. But between innings he told his teammates that he was hearing "pretty music."

That night a local sportswriter came up to Newsom with a pretty girl. "Bobo," he said proudly, "I just got married. Meet my wife."

"A pleasure, my dear madam," said Bobo, bowing gallantly and flicking the ashes off his cigar. "By the way, would you like to feel the bump on my head?" He thrust his forehead toward the startled girl. She touched the bump hesitantly. Then Bobo bowed again and went on his way.

"Don't mind him," said the sportswriter, sighing. "Newsom's really a nice guy. He's just a little bit crazy, that's all."

It seemed that baseballs were always colliding with Bobo Newsom. Sometimes it was his own fault. In 1935 he was pitching against the Cleveland Indians, and up stepped Earl Averill, one of the best hitters in the American League. Bobo quickly slipped over two strikes.

"Hey, Earl, watch this next pitch," Newsom called out. "I'm gonna put it over the outside corner, waist-high."

Averill dug in and waved his bat menacingly.

58 : BASEBALL'S ZANIEST STARS

Sure enough, Newsom threw a fast ball over the outside corner, waist high. Averill swung viciously. The ball rocketed right back at Newsom and hit him on the leg. The talkative pitcher hobbled after the ball, got it and threw out the batter by a half-step.

"Are you okay, Bobo?" asked the club trainer, reaching down to examine the injury.

"Get back to the bench," ordered Newsom, turning away.

He hung in there and finished the ballgame. Then he limped back to the dressing room. "Doc," he told the trainer, "I think ol' Bobo's leg is busted."

An X-ray showed that Newsom had a broken bone in his kneecap. Yet he had pitched most of the game on one good leg! He was out of action for five weeks.

Henry Louis Newsom, the son of a farmer named Henry Quillan Buffkin Newsom, was born in Hartsville, South Carolina, on August 11th. What year? The record books say it was 1907, but nobody is really sure, because Newsom kept giving different dates to all the sportswriters. Sometimes it was 1906, or 1908, or 1905, or 1907. It all depended on what kind of mood he was in. He would make himself older or younger according to how he felt that day.

His uncle Jake nicknamed him "Buck" when Newsom was still a tiny tot, and a good many people used that nickname. But the story goes that he could not pronounce the name Buck; the best he could manage was "Bo." Later he added another "Bo" and became known as "Bobo" most of the time.

Not only did the big hurler call himself Bobo, but he called everyone else Bobo as well. "Hey, Bobo," he might say to a teammate, "you looked real good out there. And when Bobo says that Bobo looked good, you can believe it." Then he would stride away, leaving the teammate scratching his head, wondering what Newsom had *really* said.

Bobo broke into organized baseball in 1928, pitching for Greenville, North Carolina. Minor league players got very little money in those days. A player was lucky to earn as much as $150 a month and many received less. Newsom made a deal with his manager, Hal Weaver. He lived at the manager's house and paid for his room but got his meals free. The men became friends, although no one could tell from the way they acted. At the dinner table Weaver would complain that Newsom was eating too much, and Newsom would tell his landlord to go soak his head. Then they would punch each other, roll around on the lawn and raise a fearful racket. Then the manager would get a catcher's mitt and Newsom would practice his pitching form.

The following season Bobo received a tryout with the Brooklyn Dodgers. In 1929 and 1930 he appeared in a total of five games for the Dodgers, winning none and losing three.

Bobo was supposed to pitch for the Chicago

Cubs in 1932 but didn't see much action there either. First he drove his car off an embankment and broke his leg. After the limb had mended, he went to a farmers' mule auction. He got too close to one of the stubborn creatures, which promptly kicked him in the same leg and broke it all over again!

Meanwhile Newsom was spending his time pitching in the minors. The record book notes that one year he pitched in the Pacific Coast League, winning 30 games and losing 11. Bobo disputed that, stoutly maintaining that he won 32 or 33.

"Listen, Bobo," he said heatedly to one sportswriter who asked about his record, "who are you gonna believe, a record book or ol' Bobo?"

Finally, in 1934, he began to pitch regularly in the major leagues, beginning with the St. Louis Browns. That was the start of his journey around baseball cities. In time Bobo Newsom became the most-traded player in the history of baseball. During his career he played with nine different teams: with the Washington Senators five different times, with the St. Louis Browns three times, the Brooklyn Dodgers and Philadelphia Athletics twice, and also once each with the New York Giants, New York Yankees, Chicago Cubs, Detroit Tigers and Boston Red Sox.

Bobo's travels soon got to be one of baseball's greatest jokes, especially where Newsom and the Washington Senators were concerned. Every few years owner Clark Griffith would buy Newsom or trade for him, and the price would be cheap. Usually the other teams were tired of Bobo's shenanigans or tired of paying his big salary. After a season or two, Griffith would trade the pitcher away, usually making a good profit.

Bobo had a great affection for Griffith and tried to do all sorts of favors for his off-again, on-again boss. "Listen, Bobo," he said to Griffith once when Newsom was pitching for Detroit, "I know business is bad, right?" Griffith mournfully nodded. "Okay. Just tell the sportswriters I'm gonna beat the pants off you guys. So the fans will come out to the park."

Griffith didn't think that was good publicity, but said he'd think it over. However, as things turned out, the Washington owner didn't have to say very much. That day Bobo got into an argument with a Washington sportswriter. Finally the writer tried to pick a fight. Bobo was drinking a bottle of pop at the time. With one hand he held the sportswriter at bay, and when he had finished his drink, he shoved the attacker off. The story was printed in the paper, and the following day a good crowd was on hand to see Newsom pitch. They hooted and jeered throughout the game, but that didn't bother Bobo. Flashing great form he pitched a two-hitter, and as the final out was made he turned, thumbed his nose at the fans and walked off the field.

Not all sportswriters were angry at Newsom. When things were dull, Bobo usually did something to liven up the day. One hot afternoon he walked out to the mound with a bunch of leaves sticking out from under his baseball cap.

"What's the big idea?" asked the plate umpire suspiciously.

"Ol' Bobo's smart," said Newsom boastfully. "See these leaves? They'll prevent me from getting sunstroke."

"I don't think the leaves will help," muttered the ump, turning away. "I believe ol' Bobo already has sunstroke."

On another occasion Bobo was listening to a discussion about Joe DiMaggio, the great Yankee center fielder, who was then terrorizing pitchers throughout the American League.

"Forget about him," interjected Newsom, who was scheduled to face the Yankees that day. "Ol' Bobo knows DiMaggio's weakness."

The first time DiMaggio faced Newsom, he smacked a double. The second time he drew a base on balls. In his third at-bat Joe bombed another two-bagger. His last time up he hit a third double.

After the game a sportswriter cornered Newsom in the dressing room. "What happened," he asked. "I thought you said you knew DiMaggio's weakness."

"I sure do, Bobo," Newsom growled. "His weakness is two-base hits!"

In 1937 Newsom was with the Boston Red Sox. To amuse himself he bought a few rabbits, which he kept in his hotel room. When the team went on a short road trip, Newsom forgot all about the bunnies. He returned to find that the creatures had eaten some of the drapes, part of the bed spread, some furniture coverings and a few other assorted bits of cloth and wood. The Red Sox management got a big bill from the hotel.

In spite of the fact that he won thirteen games for the Red Sox that year, the club had had enough of him. He was traded away to the St. Louis Browns at the end of the season.

Before the start of the 1938 season, the owner of the Browns had a talk with his star pitcher. "Bobo," he said, "the manager tells me you're going to pitch the opening game. If you win it, I'll give you a bonus—money for a new suit of clothes."

Bobo grunted and went back to his practice. He pitched the opening game and won it. After the game the club owner came up to Newsom.

"I keep my promises," he said, taking out a roll of bills.

"Keep the money!" said Newsom. "I already bought the suit yesterday. You'll find the bill on your desk."

That year Bobo Newsom pitched his heart out. The St. Louis Browns played terrible ball, winning only 55 games all season. Newsom won 20 games and lost 16. That year only one other pitcher in the American League won twenty games. Sometimes Bobo would start in the first game of a doubleheader and relieve in the second game. Yet, amazingly, he never came down with a sore arm. He started 40 games and completed 31

Newsom discusses baseball with his Detroit Tiger team-mate, pitcher Lynwood "Schoolboy" Rowe.

of them, pitching a total of 330 innings and facing 1,200 batters. In one game he struck out six New York Yankees in succession. Yet, shortly after the 1939 season opened, he was traded to the Detroit Tigers.

After winning 17 games with Detroit over part of 1939, Bobo really took the American League apart in 1940. He chalked up 13 victories in a row as the Tigers began a march toward the pennant. Hoping to rack up number fourteen, Bobo started against the Red Sox and came to grief very quickly. Ted Williams of the Red Sox hit a slow hopper down the first base line, and Newsom ran over to field it. He caught the ball and jammed it against Williams, breaking his thumb.

The injured hand was placed in a cast. But Bobo wasn't the kind to sit around moaning. The cast was off in a week, and a couple of days later he took his turn on the mound. Bobo lost a close game to the Athletics and his victory streak was broken.

The Tigers won the pennant that year, finishing one game ahead of Cleveland. Bobo won 21 and lost only five. Naturally he was named to pitch the first game of the World Series against the Cincinnati Reds. To celebrate the occasion, Bobo invited some friends and relatives, including his father. Bobo won in a breeze, beating the Reds' Paul Derringer by a score of 7-2. He allowed only eight hits and was never in trouble at any time.

However, the excitement was too much for his father, who suffered a heart attack and died suddenly. Sadly, Bobo went home to South Carolina for the funeral.

When he rejoined the team, Bobo Newsom looked grim, determined. He didn't seem to have any fun left in him. And he announced to a couple of sportswriters before the fifth game, "Ol' Bobo's gonna win this ballgame for Dad."

Few pitchers could have beaten Henry Louis Newsom that day. He was terrific. The Tigers won, 8-0. And while shutting out the Reds, Bobo allowed only three hits and struck out seven batters.

Cincinnati won the sixth game and the series was tied at three games each. With very little rest,

Newsom was named to pitch the deciding seventh game.

"Are you going to win this game for your dad too?" Newsom was asked.

"Nope. Gonna win now for ol' Bobo," was the reply.

It was a marvelous pitchers' battle, with Newsom and Derringer fighting each batter, getting out of one jam after another. Detroit led, 1-0, until the bottom of the seventh.

Then Cincinnati's Frank McCormick cracked a two-bagger. Jimmy Ripple hit a fly ball and McCormick held up between second and third base to see if it would be caught. The ball hit the top of the fence and bounced back into the playing field. A fast relay brought the ball to Detroit shortstop Dick Bartell, who whirled toward home. He seemed to hesitate as McCormick rounded third and headed home. Bartell's throw was too late, and Ripple went to third base. He scored later on a fly ball, giving Cincinnati the lead, 2-1.

And that was how the game ended. Both Newsom and Derringer each allowed only seven base hits. Perhaps some faster fielding on the part of Bartell would have kept McCormick from scoring. But that is merely second-guessing.

Such great pitching deserved to be rewarded, and the Tigers made sure Bobo was well-paid the following year. He was given a salary of $35,000, which was a great deal of money in those days. Bobo began to spend it almost immediately. He showed up at training camp driving a huge car which was equipped with a horn that played "Hold That Tiger!"—a popular song of that era. When the team came home to Detroit, Bobo reserved a table in a Detroit hotel's dining room for the entire season, so that he and his friends would always have a place to feast on rich food and champagne.

But Newsom didn't do as well on the field as he did at the table. That year Newsom lost twenty games, winning only a dozen. And he was traded again—back to the Washington Senators.

Through the years of World War II Newsom bounced around from one team to another, in both leagues. Starting 1942 with the Senators, he went to the Brooklyn Dodgers, then to the St. Louis Browns, back to the Senators and finally to the Philadelphia Athletics.

And always Bobo remained the same. The sportswriters could turn to him for a funny story or two, so that the American people could forget about the grim war headlines for a few moments. Newsom claimed that he had developed some "new" pitches. One was the "V for Victory" pitch. How was it thrown? Bobo claimed that was a military secret, but he guaranteed that it would strike out opposing batters.

Another was his "triple-windup Ephus ball." Bobo would go into his pitching windup and pump once, twice, three times, then rear back as though he intended to fire a terrific fast ball. But the ball would leave his hand as if it were sailing in slow motion. It floated high into the air, then

After another trade, Newsom warms up for the Yankees.

descended slowly, looking like a big fat balloon.
Bobo didn't throw it very often, perhaps once or
twice in a game, and the batters seldom swung at
it. More often than not it was outside the strike

zone. Even Newsom admitted he wasn't sure where the ball would go.

In 1947 the New York Yankees wanted some pitching insurance, and they purchased Newsom from Washington, where he had already won four games. By that time he was *really* "ol' Bobo," being almost forty years of age. His fast ball was just a fond memory, but Bobo knew how to mix his curves and off-speed pitches so that he could still fool a lot of batters. Indeed, he won seven games with the Yanks.

In a game against the White Sox Bobo went to bat against Joe Haynes. He swung and topped the ball. It dribbled back to the pitcher. Bobo realized he was out by a city block. Instead of running to first, he dropped the bat and began to stroll toward the dugout.

But Haynes didn't throw to first. He just stood there, holding the ball and watching Bobo, a puckish grin on his face. When Bobo heard the crowd start to laugh, he turned to see what was the cause of the merriment. Of course he was already automatically out because he had gone far out of the base line. But evidently the umpires were enjoying the situation as much as Haynes and the fans.

Bobo and Haynes stared at each other for a couple of seconds. Then Bobo started to walk toward first. So did Haynes. Bobo noticed that Rudy York, the Chicago first baseman, was a few feet off the bag, laughing so hard that he was hardly able to stand up. Suddenly Bobo made a dash toward first. So did Haynes. So did York. At the last possible moment Haynes tossed the ball to York, who stepped on first to retire the batter.

That year the Yanks won the flag by twelve games. Although he had not been with the Yankees for the full season, the players voted him a three-quarter share of the World Series money. Bobo didn't think that was enough. He said disgustedly, "Maybe they should make my championship ring three-quarter size too!"

Like nearly all ball players, Newsom was extremely superstitious. One of the best examples of his fears was an incident that took place in 1951. He was temporarily out of the majors, pitching for Birmingham of the Southern Association.

In a game against Little Rock Bobo put the side out in order the first inning. As he was taking his warmup pitches for the second inning, a man suddenly leaped out of the stands and ran to the plate. He was holding a black cat. As Newsom stood on the mound dumbstruck, the man waved the cat in front of Bobo, then ran back to his seat.

Completely unsettled, Bobo issued three walks and allowed three hits. Little Rock scored four runs. As Bobo was walking back to the dugout, some lady spectators began scattering pieces of paper in his path. They knew that was another of Bobo's pet superstitions. And when Bobo went out to the mound again for the third inning, there was the man with the black cat again. Disgustedly, Bobo stomped off the mound, hurled his glove into the grandstand and went to the showers.

Bobo also refused to tie his own shoelaces on the day he was scheduled to pitch. He would suit up and then stand in the middle of the dressing room without saying a word, until someone kneeled down and tied them.

From 1948 until 1952 Newsom pitched minor league ball. But he still wanted one more shot at the majors. His old standby, Clark Griffith of the Washington Senators, rescued him again. Bobo's stuff was almost completely gone. All he had was pretty good control, a slow curve and a lot of courage. Soon even the Senators couldn't use him. Casting about for another club, Bobo settled on the Athletics. He knew that kindly old Connie Mack was a soft touch. Mack tried desperately to avoid Bobo, for he knew that Bobo could talk anybody into anything. He even insisted that Philadelphia coach Earl Brucker stay with him, so that he wouldn't weaken and give Newsom a job. But Bobo used all his persuasive powers and soon he was on the Philadelphia pitching staff.

In 1953 Bobo Newsom won two ball games. As he walked off the mound after his second victory, he said to Connie Mack, "This is it, Bobo. I'm finished. And thanks for everything. I don't think you can afford Bobo's salary any more."

Mack understood. The talkative pitcher had just wanted a chance to win his 200th game in the American League. It didn't matter that he had also won eleven games in the National League. He considered himself an American Leaguer, first, last and always.

Late in his career, Newsom puts on another uniform and pitches for the Philadelphia Athletics.

Henry Louis "Bobo" Newsom was certainly a colorful player; but he was also one of baseball's better pitchers. He lasted twenty years in the big leagues, winning 211 games and losing 222. Most of the time he was with second-division teams, and more often than not he lost games that pitchers with better teams would have won. Twice he pitched both games in a doubleheader, because his team just didn't have another pitcher ready to start.

Bobo even claimed he had pitched a no-hitter, although it isn't officially listed in the record books. Facing the Red Sox, he blazed his way through the Boston lineup for nine innings without allowing a hit. But, in the tenth inning, two walks and a scratch single beat him, 2-1. Newsom always claimed that baseball was usually a nine-inning game and that he should be credited with a no-hitter.

"Was that the only one you ever pitched?" someone asked.

"Yeah," sighed Bobo. "They don't grow in bunches like bananas."

Neither do ball players like Bobo Newsom.

5/Dizzy Dean
and the Gas House Gang

It was high noon, and the dining room at Philadelphia's Bellevue-Stratford Hotel was quite crowded. Waitresses scurried to and from the kitchen, bringing in trays of lunches. Suddenly three men walked into the room. They wore caps and overalls, and carried buckets of paint, brushes and ladders.

"Isn't this place ready yet?" demanded one of the painters disgustedly.

Three members of the Gas House Gang, as the St. Louis Cardinals were called in the 1930s: pitcher Dizzy Dean (far left), his brother Daffy (left) and third baseman Pepper Martin.

"There's supposed to be a banquet here tonight, and we've got to have the room all painted by then," said another.

"Leave it to me," said the third. "I'll get the room cleared." Then he called out in a loud voice, "Ladies and gentlemen, there has been a mistake. Will you please leave the dining room. We must begin painting right away."

As the puzzled patrons began to call their waitresses, the painter added, "It's all right, you don't have to pay your checks. The management wants to apologize and hopes you'll come back another day."

The customers walked out, and the painters began to shove the tables and chairs to one side. They set up ladders and spread out tarpaulins. Then they walked out of the dining room too.

Hours passed and the painters didn't return. The hotel manager was called. Painters? A banquet? No checks for the customers? Was everybody in the hotel crazy?

Finally the manager got to the bottom of the mystery. The "painters" were three baseball players with the St. Louis Cardinals—Dizzy Dean, his brother Daffy and Pepper Martin. The irate manager went screaming to the Cardinals' management, and the prank cost the team several thousand dollars. Furthermore the Cardinals were told that they would no longer be welcome at the Bellevue-Stratford Hotel.

The Cardinals' general manager, Branch Rickey, gave the players a stern lecture when they returned to St. Louis. But in his heart he knew it was useless. Nearly every member of the team was a little crazy, and they were always finding new ways to irritate the team's management.

The ringleader of this rowdy crew was a right-handed pitcher named Jerome Herman "Dizzy" Dean. He earned his nickname, not because of his nutty antics, but because of the way he pitched. A sportswriter once wrote that opposing batters got dizzy swinging at his fast ball and that's how his nickname started. But fans soon realized that he was as dizzy as the batters.

Dizzy Dean was born on a farm in Lucas, Arkansas, on January 11, 1911. Like many other teen-agers, he began his career by pitching for local teams, and by the time he was nineteen, Diz was pitching for St. Joseph, Missouri, down in the minor leagues.

Life was a ball for Diz in those days. Because he liked to stay out late, he kept rooms in several local hotels just to make sure he'd have a place to sleep no matter where he was. But his night life didn't seem to hurt his pitching, for he won about seventeen games with St. Joseph. Before the season was over, he was called up to Houston of the Texas League.

Dizzy won his first game for Houston, 12-1. The following morning he was standing in the office of club owner Fred Ankenman, a sheepish look on his face. "Mr. Ankenman, ah'd like to apologize fer what happened in that ball game. Ah shore am sorry, an' effen ah git another chance, ah promise it won't happen no more," said Dizzy in his back-woods accent.

Ankenman scratched his head. "All right, you're forgiven," he said. "But first tell me, what did you do wrong?"

"Ah let 'em score. Can you imagine them bush-ers gettin' a run offen me? Why, that's terrible!"

When the season ended for the Texas League, the major leagues were still in operation. Dizzy was called up by the Cardinals. Their manager, Gabby Street, wanted to see what this hot-shot young pitcher had to offer. And Diz showed plenty! He pitched a three-hit victory over the

Pittsburgh Pirates. Street was elated, and Diz was told to report to the Cardinals at their spring training camp the following year.

No doubt Diz was pleased at the prospect of making the majors so quickly. But he never did like the hard work and discipline of a major league training camp. The first day he showed up on time. The second day he was a few minutes late. And the third day he just stayed in bed and slept. Gabby Street was in a rage and told the rookie to turn in his uniform. But Diz had a way of talking himself out of trouble, and he convinced Street to give him another chance.

Still, Diz kept getting into one jam after another. He was late for practice, he criticized the way the starting pitchers were throwing. He had a talent for speaking up at the wrong time. Street kept hoping that he would shut up, but Dizzy never did.

One day the Cardinals were playing an exhibition game against Connie Mack's slugging Philadelphia Athletics. The A's began to tee off early and they seemed to be able to score whenever they pleased.

Dean was sitting near the manager in the dugout. He looked sadly at the Cardinal pitcher and finally said, "Ah shore wish ah could fog in a few agin' them fellers." Street tried to ignore the brash rookie. But Dean began to make a pest of himself, and finally the manager could take no more.

"All right!" he snarled. "You want to pitch? Go

Still under 20 years old, Dizzy Dean poses in a minor league uniform.

ahead. Don't warm up, just go out there, pick up the ball and start throwing."

As Dean trotted happily toward the mound, Street muttered to himself, "He asked for it. Now he'll learn his lesson!"

Dean was about to face three of the greatest batters in baseball history: Al Simmons, Jimmy Foxx and Mickey Cochrane. The previous year, 1930, Simmons had hit .381, Jimmy "Double-X" Foxx had hit .335, and Cochrane—considered by many to have been the greatest catcher ever to play in the majors—batted .357. Now the inexperienced rookie was facing them with nobody out and the bases loaded!

Any pitcher with a grain of sense would have been terrified. Perhaps Dizzy didn't really know who they were; maybe he didn't particularly care who they were. But his fastball was working and he struck out all three of them!

As Dean strutted back to the bench, he told Gabby Street, "You shore are lucky ah'm playin' on yore side, skipper."

That night Dean was on a train, headed back to Houston.

"I could have kept him," said Street later. "But he was too cocky for his own good. The way he was talking to the veterans, somebody was bound to punch him in the nose sooner or later. Maybe the whole team would have pounced on him. I couldn't sacrifice the good of the club for one rookie pitcher."

Diz had another winning year in the minors, and in 1932 he was back with the Cardinals, this time to stay. But Street was right about one thing. Dizzy was always getting into hot water with his teammates. For instance, Diz would wear one shirt until the dirt could almost be scraped off with a knife. Then he threw it away. And quite often he was caught wearing his roommate's silk shirts.

"Diz, leave my shirts alone!" roared his roommate.

"Now now, you shouldn't feel like that, pal," replied Diz. "Do you want the team t'be ashamed of me? How would it look effen ah walked aroun' with bad-lookin' clothes? Ah'm doin' the team a favor."

In his first year with the Cards, Diz proved he was a great pitcher by winning eighteen games. He pitched more innings and struck out more batters than any other National League pitcher. In spite of his efforts, the team tumbled from first place to sixth. And when the team was still bogged down the following season, Gabby Street was fired. Replacing him was the great St. Louis second baseman, Frankie Frisch, the "Fordham Flash."

What a collection of colorful players were those men of the 1934 Cardinals! At shortstop was Leo "Lippy" Durocher, a brash, talkative firebrand, who was happy only when he was giving the umpires or his opponents a hard time. Once, when Leo was with the Yankees, he saw a huge mountain of a man named Bob Fothergill coming to the plate. Fothergill was a good hitter, but he was also one of the fattest players in the game. In fact "Fatty" was his nickname, and how he hated it! Leo knew how sensitive he was, and as Fothergill tapped the dirt from his spikes, Lippy suddenly cried out, "Stop the game!"

"Lippy" Leo Durocher in a Brooklyn uniform shortly after leaving St. Louis. He later managed several teams including the Cubs.

"What's the matter?" asked umpire Harry Geisel.

"What's the *matter*? Ump, don't you know the rules?" snapped Leo, pointing at Fothergill. "*Both* those guys can't bat at the same time!"

Fothergill was so mad he couldn't control his swings, and he struck out.

On another occasion Leo got into an argument with umpire "Beans" Reardon. He said a few unkind words, and finally Reardon barked, "Durocher, one more insult and you're out of the game!"

Leo turned away, muttering under his breath. "What's that you said?" growled the umpire.

"Didn't you hear me?" asked Lippy sweetly. "Then try to guess. You've been guessing at balls and strikes all afternoon." And before Leo could say another sentence, he was thumbed out of the game.

Playing third base was a hard-charging, scrappy guy named John Leonard "Pepper" Martin. Pepper had come to the Cardinals a few years earlier and had been the star of the 1931 World Series. He was an outfielder then but was converted into a third baseman.

Pepper was the kind of all-out player that managers dream about. When he slid into a base, it was with a head-first dive. When a ground ball came his way, he blocked it with his chest, his arms, his legs—or any other part of his body that was handy. Pop flies were his meat and potatoes. If he thought he had a chance to grab one, he would race all the way to first base, and if anyone happened to be in his path, look out! In self-defense the St. Louis infield had to appoint one player to direct traffic on all popups. Otherwise Pepper would have knocked down his teammates like ten-pins.

Branch Rickey, the Cardinal general manager, loved to invent stories about Pepper Martin. "Do you know how fast he is?" Rickey would say. I'll tell you. When Pepper goes rabbit hunting, he won't settle for any skinny ones. He chases the rabbit, catches up and then runs alongside it. He reaches down to feel how fat it is. If the rabbit is fat enough, he stoops down and grabs it. That's how fast Pepper Martin is."

Pepper teased everyone who came his way, including Dizzy. Not many batters bothered Dean, but one who seemed to hit him at will was the New York Giants' first baseman, Bill Terry. Of course Terry also made life miserable for most other pitchers. His lifetime batting average was .341.

In one game Terry began knocking drives right back through the box. One hard shot hit Dizzy on the shins, and another hot grounder almost tore Dean's glove off his hand. When Terry came up for the third time, Pepper called time out and strolled over to the pitcher.

"Diz, I've got some good advice. Care to listen?"

"Why, shore," said Dizzy affably. "What's the good advice?"

"I don't think you're playing deep enough to field Terry's hits," grinned Pepper, beating a hasty retreat to third base.

In many ways manager Frankie Frisch was as zany as any other player on the team. Frankie had a marvelous time picking on umpires, but he tried not to be crude about it. Once when an umpire made a decision that Frankie thought was wrong, he walked over to him with a look of concern on his face.

"Oh, you poor man," he said, his voice full of pity. "I know what's wrong. You're old and your eyes are not as good as they used to be. Maybe a pair of glasses would stop the headaches. I know a very good eye doctor, and I'll give you his card after the game."

Also on the club was Paul Dean, Dizzy's younger brother. It was only right that he was given the nickname "Daffy" when he came to the Cards. Daffy was somewhat quieter than Dizzy—but not much. And it seemed that odd things naturally happened when he was pitching.

In one game a young lady leaped out of the stands and ran up to the plate. She grabbed a bat that had been left lying there and stepped into the batter's box to face Daffy. For some reason nobody bothered her. So Daffy lobbed one in to her, and she swung and tapped the ball back to him. Then she dropped the bat and went scurrying toward first base. Daffy was grinning from ear to ear as he picked up the ball, but he didn't throw it to first.

"Ah guess," he chortled later, "ah'm the only pitcher in history which ever allowed a base hit by a lady batter!"

Any stranger wandering around the St. Louis dugout in 1935 would surely think he had blundered into an insane asylum. Many of the players chewed tobacco, and the stranger would have to be alert to avoid being sprayed by tobacco juice. If he tried to interview Dizzy, or Lippy, or Daffy, or Pepper, he would find that *they* were asking the questions and also answering them. Then he would probably wonder at the strange noise coming from the dugout or the locker room sounding a little bit like music. He would find out that the noise came from that fabulous musical group, "The Mudcatters," which consisted of Dizzy, Daffy, Pepper and Ducky Medwick. The "instruments" they used were a washboard, a kazoo, an old whiskey jug and a musical saw. When they all cranked up together, they sounded like four cats with their tails caught in a meat grinder. They played mostly country music, but they also played songs that they made up as they went along.

Most of the Cardinals were superstitious. Once Pepper Martin was in a bad slump, and it seemed that nothing could shake him out of it. Knowing how superstitious Pepper was, Frisch hit on an idea. He bought a few dozen pins and scattered them in front of the hotel elevator when he thought Pepper was coming down to the lobby. Ball players believed it was good luck to find a pin.

However Ducky Medwick came out of the elevator first. He saw the pins, and with a glad cry knelt down and began to gather them up.

"Leave them alone!" pleaded Frisch. "I left them there for Pepper to find."

"Oh, yeah?" sneered Ducky. "Let Martin find his own pins!"

But in the end it was Jerome Herman Dean who was the nuttiest of them all. There was no telling what he would do next. For instance, one blistering hot afternoon in St. Louis, when the temperature climbed above 100 degrees, Dizzy lit a bonfire to warm his hands. And when that didn't seem to work, he put on a heavy winter overcoat.

Because he was a naturally friendly soul, Diz would often visit with rival teams in their locker room. The players liked Diz well enough, but sometimes the situation could get sticky. One time Diz was still in the Boston Braves' locker room while their manager, Bill McKechnie, was going over the strategy the team would use against the Cardinals that afternoon. It was only when the meeting broke up that McKechnie spotted Diz.

"What are you doing here, Dean? Spying on us?" McKechnie asked.

"Now, don't get yourself so worked up," soothed Dizzy. "Ah'm jes' tryin' t'help out. An' lemme tell ya, that's smart stuff ya worked out. Except one man, an' that's Pepper Martin. Effen ah was you, ah'd play him more aroun' toward left. Pepper likes to pull the ball."

So great was Dizzy's self-confidence that he would even give the other team some help. Before taking on the Braves one afternoon, he ambled over to the dugout and told them, "No curves from ol' Diz today, fellers. Only fast balls."

Diz threw only blazers. He allowed three hits as the Cards won, 1-0!

Vince DiMaggio, brother of Joe and Dom DiMaggio, was also a major leaguer but wasn't nearly as good a hitter as his brothers. He swung from the heels all the time and consequently struck out a lot. Diz bet Vince that he could strike him out every time they faced each other.

"Let's make it 25 cents every time at bat, Vinnie ol' pal," Diz challenged.

The bet was made. Three straight times Vince DiMaggio struck out. The fourth time he managed to hit a high pop foul behind the plate. The catcher flipped his mask and camped under the ball.

Diz saw he was losing a chance to win another 25 cents. "Drop it! Drop it!" he screamed to his receiver. "Leave that danged ball alone!"

Startled, the catcher stepped back and let the ball drop. Dizzy breathed a sigh of relief, then burned strike three past DiMaggio.

Usually Dizzy bore down on every batter he faced. But once in a while his soft heart got the better of him. When Diz first came to the Cardinals, he sometimes roomed with an infielder named Burgess Whitehead. Later Whitehead was traded to the Giants, and when the two men faced each other, Diz decided to go easy on his former pal.

He served up a nice, fat pitch, right over the heart of the plate, belt high. Whitehead ripped a line drive that zoomed right back at Dizzy, hit his head and bounced into the outfield. Dizzy fell, and all his teammates rushed out to see if he was alive or dead. Daffy reached him ahead of the others. He saw that his brother was blinking rapidly, cross-eyed, with a vacant look.

"Yer all right," said Daffy. "It was only a glancin' blow."

"Reckon so," wheezed Diz. "But ah shore won't do *that* again!"

Dizzy and Daffy Dean were fantastic in 1934, as the Cardinals won the pennant on the last day of the season. Dizzy won 30 games, losing only seven; Daffy won 19 and had eleven defeats. The brothers won a total of 49 games while the rest of the

Dizzy Dean warms up for the Cardinals in 1934.

Cardinal pitching staff put together managed to win only 46.

The high point of the year for Dizzy and Daffy came in a doubleheader against the Brooklyn Dodgers. Before the first game, Frisch went over the Brooklyn lineup with Dizzy.

"Cuccinello gets only outside curve balls," ordered Frisch.

"What for?" asked Dizzy.

"Because I said so!" roared the exasperated Frisch. "And keep the ball low and outside for Sam Leslie."

As Frisch went over the Dodger lineup man by man, Diz grew impatient and finally he stopped the manager.

"Listen, Frankie," he said, shaking his head, "I already won twenty-six games so far. How does it look for an infielder like you tellin' a star pitcher like me how to pitch?"

"Okay, do it your own way," said Frisch angrily. "And I hope they pin your ears back!"

Dean proceeded to set the Dodgers on their ears. It wasn't until the eighth inning that they got a hit, and Diz closed out the day with a two-hitter.

Daffy Dean surpassed even that gaudy performance. In the second game he hurled a no-hitter. Nobody was happier about it than big brother Dizzy. He hugged Paul fiercely and yelled, "Shucks, why didn't you tell me you was gonna do that? Ah'd have done it too."

Dizzy took great pride in his brother's efforts,

and Daffy felt the same way about Dizzy. "Me'n Paul, we'll win this here World Series," trumpeted Dizzy.

In the Series the Cards faced the Detroit Tigers. Diz pitched the first game and won, 8-3. Detroit's Schoolboy Rowe won the second contest, but Daffy came back with a victory in game number three.

In the fourth game there were a few fireworks —but they were all inside Dizzy Dean's head. Diz entered the game as a pinch runner at first base. The next batter, Pepper Martin, hit a hard grounder that looked like a sure double play. The ball was thrown to second and Diz was forced out. Then, as the ball was thrown toward first, Diz seemed to straighten up or even to jump. The ball hit him smack on the head, and he dropped as though a truck had run over him.

When Diz regained consciousness, the first question he asked was, "Did they double up Pepper? Was he safe?"

"Are you hurt, Dizzy?" asked the anxious trainer.

Dizzy curled his lip in a sneer. "Now you know you can't hurt ol' Diz with a hit in the head. Ah didn't even know ah got hit. All ah saw was a lovely moon, an' some stars, an' some rockets goin' off in pretty colors."

The Cards lost the game. Diz tried to get the team back on the track again in the fifth game. But he was beaten on a home run by the peerless Detroit second baseman, Charlie Gehringer.

The Gas House Gang refused to quit. Daffy pitched and won the sixth game to tie up the series again. In the seventh game Dizzy Dean took the hill. And nobody could touch him. The Cardinals scored seven runs in the third inning and coasted to victory.

Late in the game Dizzy got silly again. Hank Greenberg, Detroit's home run-hitting first baseman, came up. Card catcher Bill Delancey flashed a few signs, but Diz kept shaking them off. Finally Frankie Frisch trotted to the mound.

"Diz," said Frisch wearily, "it's been a long season. We're all tired. Don't start fooling around now. Tell your old buddy what's wrong?"

"What did you say I *shouldn't* throw to this feller?" asked Diz thoughtfully.

"Don't throw him a fast ball on the outside," said Frisch. "If you do, he's liable to knock it into the Pacific Ocean."

"Ah think yore wrong, Frankie," replied Diz stoutly. "Jes' watch this!"

Diz fired his best fast ball. He threw it high and outside, right into Greenberg's strong point. Greenberg swung with all his might and hit a hard line drive that missed Dizzy's right ear by six inches. Dizzy stood on the mound, hands on hips, and shook his head admiringly.

"Hey, Frankie, yo're right," he called out. "Greenberg murders fast balls high and outside."

Diz had an 11-0 shutout. True to his boast, "Me'n Paul" had won the World Series, each brother winning two games.

Two zany ballplayers meet: Lefty Gomez of the Yankees (left) and the Cardinals' Dizzy Dean.

Diz wanted a big raise in salary, and while owner Sam Breadon agreed he should have a raise, he didn't think Dean was entitled to $20,000. In those Depression days that was a lot of money. Diz did settle for less than $20,000, but he had to pull one last prank before giving in.

One afternoon he telephoned his boss from halfway across the country, and they talked for a long, long time. When he finished, Daffy asked him, "Did you get the $20,000?"

"Naw," said Dizzy sadly. "Ah didn't expect to, neither." Then he brightened. And he began to laugh. "Jerome, what's so funny?" he asked.

"Why are you laughing if you didn't get the big raise?"

"Well," gasped Diz, wiping the tears from his eyes, "y'know we kept on talkin' fer a long time. Wait till he gets the phone bill. Ah reversed the charges on him!"

After winning thirty games in 1934, Diz kept up his winning ways for a few years. The following season he won 28, and in 1936 he had 24 victories. Daffy wasn't as fortunate. He won nineteen games again in 1935, but then developed a sore arm and won only a dozen more games during the rest of his career.

Disaster struck Dizzy Dean in 1937. He had already won twelve games by the time of the All Star game. He was pitching against the American League when a line drive struck his foot, breaking the big toe. Always a great fighter, Diz tried to come back too soon, while his toe was still bandaged. Pitching with an unnatural motion, he hurt his arm and was never the same.

The Cards then sold Dean to the Chicago Cubs for $185,000 plus two pitchers. Cub owner Phil Wrigley, whose real business was making chewing gum, was told that Dean had a bad arm and would no longer be effective.

"I know," said Wrigley. "But fans will still pay to see Dizzy Dean pitch. I'll get my money back at the box office. You'll see."

Wrigley was right. Diz managed to win seven ballgames for the Cubs in 1938, which helped them win the National League pennant. In the

World Series Diz held off the mighty New York Yankees for seven innings. In the eighth Frank Crosetti and Joe DiMaggio each hit homers with a man on base, and Diz was done. But he had gone up against the Yanks with no fast ball at all, just some sidearm curves—and a lot of courage.

Old-time baseball fans are sentimental people. They like to talk about the great players of the past as if they were knights in shining armor. If the Cardinals were knights, Frankie Frisch was Merlin the Magician, allowing his team to have fun and win games at the same time. Frankie's warriors were Ducky Medwick, Ripper Collins and Pepper Martin. They scored the runs, pounding the enemy pitchers into submission. Leo Durocher was the first line of defense, making amazing plays around shortstop, gobbling up every ground ball that came within reach.

And as for Dizzy Dean—he was the court jester.

6/Babe Herman

Most teams in the major leagues had their share of colorful players. But old-time baseball fans seem to agree that the team with the best collection of zany players was the Brooklyn Dodgers of the 1920s. In earlier days they had been called the Robins. They were soon called the Dodgers because their fans had to dodge trolleys and buses on the way to the stadium. But in the 1920s they got an even better nickname—"The Daffyness Boys." The daffiest and most colorful of them all was an outfielder named Floyd "Babe" Herman.

Whenever wacky players are mentioned, the name Babe Herman is up among the leaders. He did pull a few stunts in his time. But Herman's reputation as a baseball clown wasn't really fair. He seldom did anything comical on purpose; things just kept happening to him. Whenever anything odd or funny happened, Babe was in the middle of it.

For some reason managers would take one look at Babe Herman and immediately begin figuring out ways to get rid of him. Their eyes would pop as the line drives flew off his bat in practice. But when they watched him gallop clumsily after a fly

Babe Herman.

ball in the outfield, they would realize that he would quickly make them old and gray with worry. In the end every team decided to dump him fast, every team except Brooklyn. There he seemed to fit in very nicely.

Babe Herman was born on June 26, 1903, in Buffalo, New York. After playing with Edmonton of the Western Canada League, he showed up at the Detroit Tiger training camp in 1922. At that time the fiery Ty Cobb, one of the great players of all time, was managing the Tigers. He might have hung on to Herman and taught him the A-B-Cs of fielding. But he didn't. After a short time Cobb sent the rookie on his way.

Babe ended up in Omaha in the minor leagues, where he began to tear up the opponents' pitching. Before long he was batting a hot .416. One day the owner of the Omaha club came to watch his boys play. An opposing batter raised a high pop foul that drifted close to the stands. Herman raced toward it and the owner watched in amazement as the ball came down and conked Herman on top of the head. In an instant the owner was out of his box seat and into the dugout.

"Fire that idiot at once!" he shouted.

"I can't," pleaded the manager. "How do you expect me to get rid of a man who's hitting over .400?"

"I don't care!" thundered the owner. "Nobody plays on my team when he tries to catch a fly ball with his head!"

Herman had a reasonable explanation. "I saw

the ball start to go into the stands," he said. "So I turned my back. I started to walk back to my position. The wind caught the ball and it drifted my way. The next thing I knew, it hit me on the head. That could have happened to anyone." But Herman was on his way again.

Next he turned up in Boston, but he hardly had time to unpack his bags. He remarked that he didn't like the climate in Boston anyway and soon was in the minor leagues in Atlanta.

Otto Miller, a former big league player, was managing Atlanta. He took one look at Herman's fielding and was convinced that Herman must go. Miller wanted to dismiss him the first day, but something stopped him. Perhaps he thought he was being too hasty. After all, the kid deserved to play in at least *one* game.

For five days Otto Miller kept wavering. Every time he was ready to let Herman go, Herman would come through with a clutch hit. On the fifth day, in a game against Nashville, Babe clubbed four straight hits. He would have had another in his fifth at-bat, but a youngster named Kiki Cuyler made an amazing one-handed catch to rob Herman of a double.

Later Miller patted Herman on the shoulder. "Too bad about Cuyler's catch," he said. "If the ball had dropped in, we'd have won the game."

Herman misunderstood. He thought the manager was blaming him for the loss. He got into an argument with the manager, and that did it. Once again Herman was a traveling man.

"Uncle Robbie"—Dodger manager Wilbert Robinson— holds a golf trophy, probably the only one his 1927 Dodgers won. Babe Herman is third from the right.

A couple of years later Herman was the property of the Boooklyn Dodgers. They had heard about him when he was playing with Seattle of the Pacific Coast League. Brooklyn scouts reported that Herman was knocking the hide off the ball. The Dodger manager, Wilbert Robinson, could hardly believe he was fortunate enough to buy such a slugger. But when Uncle Robbie saw Babe in practice, he could hardly believe he had made such a dreadful mistake.

In desperation Uncle Robbie even tried to give him away! But there were no takers. The Dodgers wanted to trade for a minor league flash named

Johnny Butler. They offered the minor league
club eight other players and Babe Herman. But
the club owner said no, thank you, he'd just take
the eight players and Uncle Robbie could keep
Herman. Robinson was more fortunate than he
thought, because Babe Herman became one of the
most popular players ever to play in Brooklyn.

Herman got his chance the very first season.
The Dodgers' first baseman, Jacques Fournier, an
aging veteran, hurt his leg, and Herman was
given a chance at the position.

Fournier had been a zany character himself.
Once a rookie pitcher asked him for some advice
during a game.

"Rogers Hornsby is up there," said the nervous
hurler. "That guy is a terror with the bat. What
should I throw?"

"Don't worry about it, son," said Fournier.
"Just give him a fast ball, high and inside."

The pitcher threw fast and tight, and Hornsby
smashed a line drive that almost took the third
baseman's head off his shoulders.

The young pitcher looked at Fournier accus-
ingly. "I thought you said a high fast ball was
Hornsby's weakness."

"I never said it was his weakness," replied
Fournier. "But if you pitched outside, he'd have
hit that kind of line drive at *me*. You think I want
to get killed?"

With Fournier out, Herman filled in at first
base creditably enough and also played in the
outfield. Somehow he managed to survive in the

field and he batted a good .319.

It is not known how many times Babe Herman almost got himself killed trying to field fly balls. He wasn't that bad as a fielder. But he looked clumsy, and he did lose track of the ball once in a while.

Once Herman was chasing a high fly near the foul line, and somehow he lost sight of the ball. Possibly he thought it would drop into foul territory, because he gave up trying to catch it. The ball dropped into fair territory for a two-base hit. Uncle Robbie blamed the Dodger pitchers who were right there, watching the play from the bullpen.

"Why didn't you tell him it was a fair ball?" Robbie demanded. "Couldn't you holler out and tell him where the ball was?"

No doubt Herman's great hitting made Robbie overlook his other weaknesses. On one occasion he sent Babe up to the plate with instructions to bunt. Babe dug in and blasted the first pitch over the wall for a home run. Some managers would have been furious that a player had disobeyed orders. But Robbie was less demanding.

"That's it, Babe!" he shouted as Herman rounded the bases. "You hit 'em your way, no matter what any dumbbell tells you!"

It was as a baserunner that Babe Herman achieved true immortality. One day at the end of Babe's first year, the manager noticed something. "Babe," said Robbie, "you have good speed. How come you don't steal any bases?"

Babe Herman demonstrates his legendary fielding ability.

Herman looked at him blankly. "You never told me to," he replied. In the last game of the season he stole two bases. The following year he began to show his real talent. In one game he stole second when there were already other runners on second and third.

Babe Herman's greatest feat of base running made him a household word. Brooklyn fans still talked about it years later when the Dodgers had moved to Los Angeles. In fact it is one of baseball's greatest stories—how Babe Herman tripled into a double play!

Brooklyn had the bases loaded: Hank DeBerry was on third, Dazzy Vance was on second and Chick Fewster was on first. There was one out. Babe came to bat and belted a long drive off the wall.

DeBerry scored easily. Vance, who didn't like running, rounded third, hesitated, and decided to stay where he was. Fewster had rounded second and was nearly to third when he saw Vance stop. Realizing that he couldn't go any farther, Fewster started to trot back toward second base.

But Babe Herman was tearing around the bases like an express train. As Fewster was nearing second, Herman tore past him on his way to third. With a great slide he made it—only to find that Vance was also standing on the bag. Fewster, who had not yet reached second, stood in the baseline, scratching his head, wondering what to do next.

When the third baseman got the ball, he was puzzled too. Just to play it safe, he began to tag

Herman is about to be tagged at third base. He seems to have slid in the wrong direction and missed the bag.

everyone within arm's length.

While the umpire was still trying to recover his senses and make the call, the third baseman suddenly realized that there was one Brooklyn player he hadn't tagged yet. So he ran after the bewildered Fewster, who didn't know which way to turn. The third baseman, waving the ball, chased Fewster across second base and all the way into the outfield. He finally caught up with him, and he slapped the ball against Fewster's back.

Actually Vance was safe. He didn't have to score if he didn't want to. But Herman was out because he didn't belong on the bag. And Fewster was also automatically out because Herman had passed him on the base line.

It took almost half an hour for the fans to stop laughing. And this bit of Brooklyn base-running was responsible for many jokes. One of them is about a fan who was holding a seat for a friend at the ballpark. The friend arrived after the game had started.

"Hurry up," shouted the fan as his friend climbed up the aisle. "Brooklyn has three men on base."

"Oh, yeah?" cracked the late-comer. "Which base?"

The fans came to love Babe Herman as much for his antics as for his hitting prowess. And make no mistake, Babe was pounding out base hits in every ball park visited by Brooklyn. But once again the fates were against him, and he never managed to win a batting championship. In 1929 Babe hit .381, but Lefty O'Doul batted .398! In 1930 Babe hit .393. But that was the year Bill Terry batted .401! How unlucky can a guy be?

In between base hits Babe continued to get his name in the newspapers for other things. One day Babe took his young son to the stadium. He got a good seat for the boy and told him to stay right there until he came for him. That afternoon Babe hit a home run, a triple and a single in four at-bats. When he got home, his wife asked, "Where's the boy?"

Babe had forgotten all about his son! He

rushed back to the field, and there was the lad still sitting in his seat in the almost empty stadium.

In 1931 Babe's average slipped, but at .313 he was still very good. He thought he deserved a raise. But 1931 was a bad business year and the Dodgers were almost broke. In fact they wanted to cut everyone's salary. Herman refused to sign his contract for 1932 and was finally traded to the Cincinnati Reds.

Since few managers would put up with his type of fielding, Herman began to travel again. He had remained with Brooklyn from 1926 through 1931. After one year with the Reds, he went to Chicago, then to Pittsburgh, back to Cincinnati and finally to Detroit. He played only 17 games with the Tigers and then continued his journeys in the minors, from Toledo to Syracuse to Jersey City and finally to the Hollywood Stars of the Pacific Coast League.

His fielding never improved. His bat might bring a cheer from a manager, but his fielding produced only groans.

In 1936, for example, when he was with the Reds for the second time, he was playing the outfield one day, his thoughts far from the game. The Reds' pitcher, Paul Derringer, was having a bit of difficulty on the mound. With men on first and third, Derringer committed a balk. The runner on third walked home and the man on first moved to second.

The next batter hit a line single, which Herman fielded on the first bounce. He took his time, walked in a few steps, then lobbed the ball to second. Herman had never seen the runners move up, and he thought they were still on first and third. While he was taking his time throwing to second, another run scored and the Redleg manager stomped around the dugout screaming with rage.

By the time he played for Hollywood, Babe didn't much care whether he played baseball or not. He was getting old, and he didn't have the old power any more. He was fat and out of condition.

The first time Babe suited up, he sat in the dugout while the Stars tangled with his old team, Seattle. In the ninth inning the Stars were one run behind. With two out and the bases loaded, Babe was sent up to pinch hit.

"Maybe I can't hit this kid pitcher," said Herman to his manager, "but watch how I paralyze him!"

The count went to three balls and two strikes. Babe backed out, rubbed his hands with dirt, then stepped back in. He waved his big bat back and forth, scowling menacingly at the inexperienced young pitcher. And it worked! The nervous kid wound up and threw the ball into the dirt. Babe trotted to first with a big grin as the winning run came across.

Babe got into his last games in 1945. The scene was Brooklyn, where he had achieved such great triumphs in the past. It was during World War II and nearly all the regular major leaguers were in the armed forces. The Dodgers had persuaded Babe to play for one last time. The fans rose and cheered as Babe Herman's name was announced. He tipped his cap and stepped to the plate. The pitch came in, Babe swung and cracked a clean hit to right field.

He rounded first a little too fast and saw that the ball was coming back to the infield in a hurry. He turned back toward first, got his feet tangled up—and fell flat on his face.

Same old Babe Herman! Some people never change!

Lefty Gomez.

7/Lefty Gomez

Students of show business say that there are two
kinds of funny men. One is called a comedian and
he says funny things. The other is called a comic
and he says or does things in a funny way.

Baseball has had both types of funny men. Babe
Herman was a comic, for instance. But Vernon
"Lefty" Gomez was a comedian, a man who was
always ready with a joke, a crazy quip, or a gag.
He said things that were funny.

In 1929 the New York Yankees heard about a
young southpaw who was mowing down the batters in the Pacific Coast League. He seemed to be
an ideal prospect because of his youth (he was not
quite twenty years old) and his great fast ball. Ed
Barrow, the Yankee general manager, took the
gamble and paid $50,000 for him. It turned out to
be one of the smartest deals any team ever made.
Gomez became a Yankee.

Lefty arrived from his home in Rodeo, Califor-
nia, with high hopes. But then he took one look at
the roster and he knew he was in trouble. The
Yankees had plenty of good pitchers, including
Herb Pennock, George Pipgras and Red Ruffing.
Besides, Gomez was still very inexperienced.

However, with typical good humor, he joked about his first attempts to pitch in the majors. Lefty especially liked to tell about his first game against the Tigers.

"Watch out for Charley Gehringer," said Catcher Bill Dickey.

Lefty got the side out in the first inning, although one player hit a home run.

"You did all right," said Dickey in the dugout.

"Thanks," said Lefty. "But when do I get to see this guy Charley Gehringer?"

Dickey looked at him with a blank stare and then said, "Who do you think hit that home run? *That* was Charley Gehringer!"

Later Gomez once said about the great Detroit second baseman, "That Gehringer is in a rut. He starts off the season hittin' .350 and he never moves his average up or down."

There was another story that Gomez told about his rookie year. "The other team had men on second and third," recalled Lefty. "I took a long windup and the man on third stole home, the man on second stole third. I took another long windup and the second runner stole home. After I finished my third windup, I was back in the minor leagues."

Lefty spent the 1930 season in the minors and the extra experience seemed to help. The following year, 1931, Lefty was back with the Yankees and he stayed for the next dozen years. He became an outstanding hurler, winning more than twenty games in three of the next four years.

When asked what had happened in 1933, the season he won only 16 games, Lefty had a story to tell.

Like nearly everybody in baseball, Lefty was very superstitious. In 1931 when he won 21 and lost only five, he lived in a certain apartment building near Yankee Stadium. The next year he lived in the same building and won 24 while losing seven. But in 1933 he lived somewhere else, and his record slipped to 16 victories and ten defeats.

"See?" said Lefty. "I broke the good luck myself. The next year I went back to the same apartment house, and sure enough, I had my biggest year—26 wins and five losses.

"So, in 1935 I went back to the house. There wasn't an apartment vacant. I tried living someplace else for a while. And I lost the first game I pitched. So I went back to that house and I begged, and I pleaded, and finally the manager got me into the house.

"And do you know what happened?" Lefty concluded with a sly smile. "I had a terrible year— won 13 and lost seven."

Lefty told another story about his bad season in 1935. It seemed that he was never very heavy, and that worried Ed Barrow. "Lefty, why don't you gain some weight?" he said to the southpaw. "Remember Jack Chesbro, who once won sixteen games in a row for the Yanks? I'll bet if you gained twenty pounds, you'd make the fans forget all about Chesbro."

Lefty reported to spring training camp with

Lefty Gomez pitches against the New York Giants in the 1937 World Series. He won two games for the Yanks.

twenty-three added pounds on his skinny frame, and started losing games right away. "How do you like that?" muttered the Yankee pitcher. "Barrow said the fans would forget about Jack Chesbro—and they almost forgot about Lefty Gomez!"

Lefty settled down after that and had three good seasons for the Yankees. And while Lefty was around, there was never a dull moment. Nobody knew what he was going to do or say next.

In one contest against the Red Sox Lefty suddenly stopped pitching and stared at the sky to watch a plane circling overhead. His friend Tony Lazzeri trotted over to the mound from second base.

"Hey, Lefty," he said, "there's a ball game going on, remember?"

Lefty glared at Lazzeri, trying to keep a straight face. "You take care of second base and the spaghetti," he said to Lazzeri, who was an Italian-American. "I'll take care of the pitching and the airplanes."

In another game Lefty put Lazzeri on the spot. There were runners on first and second when the batter hit a grounder right back to Lefty. Frankie Crosetti, the shortstop, rushed over to cover the bag for the double play throw. But Gomez threw the ball to Lazzeri, who was nowhere near the bag. Fortunately Lazzeri thought quickly and threw the runner out at first.

"Why did you throw it to Lazzeri?" demanded manager Joe McCarthy after the inning was over.

"Everybody's always saying that Tony Lazzeri knows what to do with the ball when he gets it. I wanted to see if he really did know."

During those golden years of Yankee victories, there was only one thing that bothered Gomez— the fact that he was such a poor hitter. Every year

Lefty and Babe Ruth had a bet on Lefty's hitting. If he got ten or more hits for the *season*, Ruth would pay him $250. But if he got fewer than ten hits, he had to pay Ruth $50. Only once did Gomez ever win the bet.

Lefty tried with all his might to look like a good hitter. On one occasion his attempt backfired painfully. He went up to the plate swinging two bats and tossed one away. Then he tapped his shoes three times with his bat to get rid of the dirt between his spikes. But on the third tap he cracked himself on the ankle so hard that he was out of action for two weeks.

One time Lefty swung from the heels and to everyone's surprise, the ball sailed far out into right field. For a moment he stood in the batter's box, amazed at his own power.

"Run, you fool!" shouted the on-deck batter.

Lefty didn't run, he trotted to first, still holding the bat and following the ball with his eyes. The ball bounced off the fence at the 340-foot sign. Lefty stepped on first and watched the right fielder chase down the ball. He never moved from the bag as the ball was picked up and relayed in to second. It was probably one of the longest singles on record.

Lefty didn't confine his sense of humor to baseball. One evening in a hotel lobby his attention was caught by a huge tank of goldfish. For a while he studied the way the fish were swimming around in the tank. Then he suddenly leaped to his feet.

"I've got a great idea," he announced to a group of Yankee players and sportswriters. "This will make my fortune. What a marvelous invention!"

"What is it, Lefty?" asked a teammate suspiciously.

"Look at those goldfish," Lefty said, pointing to the big bowl. "The young fish can swim around all they like, but what about the old goldfish? Don't you think they get tired?"

"I never thought about that," said the teammate.

"Aha, but I did! Know what my invention is? A revolving goldfish bowl, made especially for old goldfish. The fish don't have to swim around. The bowl keeps turning, and the water swims past the fish!"

With this kind of idea, it was no wonder that Lefty soon earned a new name. Sportswriters began calling him "Goofy" Gomez.

As Lefty grew older, his fast ball wasn't quite as speedy, and he had to get by more on curves and control. The big hitters were teeing off on him. But Lefty still hung in there and won his share of games.

"What's the secret of your success, Lefty?" asked a sportswriter.

"A fast outfield," replied Gomez with a straight face.

Once he faced Jimmy Foxx, one of the most feared sluggers in the game. Lefty managed to get two strikes on him. Then Foxx hammered one out of the park, foul by inches. Yankee catcher Bill Dickey squatted down and gave Lefty the sign for the next pitch. Lefty shook it off. Dickey called for another pitch. Once more Lefty shook his head. Dickey called time out and trotted to the mound.

"What do you want to throw, Lefty?" he asked.

"If it's all the same, Bill, I'd rather not throw that big gorilla anything at all," muttered Gomez.

Late in his career he was matched in a game with Bob Feller of the Cleveland Indians. Feller's amazing fast ball traveled nearly 100 miles per hour, but he was still a young pitcher and his control was not always very sharp. Late in the game the sun had gone down and it was beginning to get dark. Then Lefty came to bat. He stopped just outside the batter's box and lit a match.

"What's wrong?" laughed the umpire. "Think that'll make you see Feller's fast one better?"

"Naw," replied Lefty. "I just want to make sure Feller sees *me*."

One day before a game the Yankees were sitting around the locker room talking about baseball in general. Someone suggested that a batter could be retired with *very* slow pitches—just soft lobs right over the plate. Lefty, who was scheduled to pitch that day, thought that was an interesting idea and decided privately that he would try the slow-ball.

In the eighth inning the Yankees were ahead by nine runs. Lefty put the new pitch to work. He tossed a straight pitch right down the middle. It was the kind of pitch even a grade-school kid

Gomez makes a face to intimidate the batter.

could have knocked a mile. The batter swung and sent a vicious line drive to the outfield. The ball never rose higher than five feet off the ground, but it sailed directly at outfielder Tommy Henrich, who didn't have to move an inch to make the putout.

Lefty threw another blooper pitch to the next hitter. The result was a long drive to deep center. Joe DiMaggio loped back to the 400-foot mark and hauled in the drive. Lefty threw a third blooper pitch and the third batter hit a sizzling grounder to Phil Rizzuto at shortstop. Li'l Phil scooped it up and flipped to first. The ball was hit so hard that the batter was out by fifteen feet. Lefty had proved that the strange pitch could get batters out, but the Yankee fielders didn't think much of the experiment.

At last the time came when Lefty couldn't put the old mustard on the fast one. "Throw harder, Lefty," the catcher pleaded.

"I'm throwing twice as hard as before," said Gomez, "but the ball's only moving half as fast."

By 1940 Lefty seemed finished. He won three and lost three. He knew that he couldn't stay with the Yankees with that kind of record. But it seemed that some other team might still be interested. The Brooklyn Dodgers were shopping around for a lefthanded pitcher and the Yankees offered Gomez. But the Dodger owner laughed when he heard the offer. "My team doesn't need that washed-up guy," he said. "Anyone who takes a chance on Gomez should jump into the river."

The Yankees decided to keep Gomez after all, and in 1941 Lefty surprised the baseball world by winning fifteen and losing five. But that was his last good year. In 1942 he won six and lost four. The next season he appeared in only one game— for the Washington Senators—and he lost that one.

Lefty Gomez will be remembered as a great pitcher. He won a total of 189 games and lost 102. He had six World Series victories and appeared in several All Star games. But he will also be remembered for his sense of humor. Even when things looked bad, Lefty somehow managed to drive away the gloom. His talent was best illustrated on one of the saddest days in Yankee history.

Since 1925 Lou Gehrig had played in 2130 consecutive games at first base for the Yankees. But during his last year Lou lost his coordination and couldn't seem to hit or field the way he used to. He soon learned that he had contracted a rare disease—a form of polio—and could not expect to live much longer. To show their appreciation to the great star, the Yankees set aside July 4th, 1940, as Gehrig Appreciation Day. Thousands of fans turned out to see the great Yankee receive many gifts from his teammates and admirers.

Gehrig made a short speech thanking the fans and the team and then trudged back to the dugout. The Yankees felt ill at ease. They all felt like crying but didn't dare break down in front of Gehrig. If he could take it, so could they.

The silence was broken by Goofy Gomez. Lefty was starting to slip in the pitching department, but his sense of humor was still working as well as ever. He moved to Gehrig's side and tapped the stricken slugger on the shoulder.

"You've got no squawk coming, Lou," said Lefty. "It took 'em fifteen years to get you out of there. These days, it only takes 'em a couple of innings with me!"

8 / A Few More Colorful Players

Why did baseball players of the past do crazy things? Today most players take the game seriously. Managers frown on any player who fools around too much, especially during a ballgame. But in earlier times many players treated baseball more as a sport than a business. They tried hard to win, but they felt they had the right to have a good time too.

One of the funniest players ever to engage in the game was Herman "Germany" Schaefer, who played for several teams including the Cubs, Tigers, Senators and Indians. Germany was versatile —he played at several positions and even tried his hand at pitching. As a batter he was never very successful. Yet, as long as he was around, things were never dull.

For instance, Germany Schaefer once stole first base! Germany was already on first base to begin with, and his teammate, Clyde Milan, was on third. The score was tied in the ninth inning and two men were out. Germany knew that Milan was pretty fast on the bases. He thought that if he tried to steal second, he might draw a throw. That would allow Milan to steal home and score the winning run.

The trouble was that the other team wasn't fooled. Germany broke for second and slid in safely. There was no throw. Milan had to stay on third.

Seeing that his strategy backfired, Germany stood up and immediately took off for first base, hoping to draw a throw. He slid in safely. Again there was no throw. But there was a great deal of confusion. Was a player permitted to go from second to first? Wasn't that the same as stealing first? And didn't the rule book say that nobody can steal first base?

Well, there was no rule against what Germany had done. Nine years earlier a player named Harry Davis had done the same thing. Nobody knew what to do then, either. Finally the major leagues made a new rule prohibiting a runner from going around the bases backward.

Schaefer was also great at handling a crowd. When they needled him, he found some way to get back at them. In a Detroit-Chicago game the Tigers were losing by one run and had a man on base. Germany was sent up to the plate as a pinch hitter. That was funny in itself because Germany was not known as a good hitter.

As he came to the batter's box, the crowd began to jeer. With great pomp and ceremony, Germany waved his bat for silence. When the crowd quieted down, he shouted at the top of his lungs, "Ladies and gentlemen, you see standing before you the world's greatest batter. I shall now give you a demonstration!"

Wonder of wonders—he hit one out of the park! As he circled the bases, the infielders heard him calling out a running commentary, as if he were announcing a horse race.

"At the quarter, Schaefer is leading by a head," he called, sliding into first base. Then he ran to second, announcing, "At the halfway point, it's Schaefer ahead by a length." And he slid into second. "It's Germany Schaefer leading by a mile," he called out as he slid into third. And as he touched home plate he turned to the fans, tipped his cap and shouted, "Ladies and gentlemen, that concludes my performance for today. I sincerely trust that you enjoyed it!"

Of course Germany wasn't always that lucky. But he did have streaks of good fortune when it seemed that everything he predicted came true. Once he was coaching at first base and he assumed a very awkward stance.

"What kind of goofy pose is that?" demanded a fan nearby.

"I always stand like this when I want the batter to hit a single," said Germany. "That's my signal to him." Sure enough, the batter got a single.

In a game against Cleveland, Germany was at his coaching post and watched the batter take two strikes. He called out to the other team's center-fielder, "Move back. This guy always hits a triple when he's got two strikes against him."

"Oh, yeah?" retorted the outfielder. "I know who's at bat. That's Hank Shanks, and he can't hit the broad side of a barn."

Shanks drove the next pitch to deepest center field and wound up on third base.

During another game Schaefer assumed another weird pose in the coaching box. He explained, "I always stand like this when I want our team to win by a score of 6-3." And the final score that day was indeed 6-3.

Germany's actions weren't always so understandable. Once he came to bat against Nick Altrock, who had a great fast ball. There was a man on first. Altrock went into his stretch, kicked high and zoomed in his blazer. Germany swung and missed. Altrock got the ball back, went into his stretch and threw to first, trying to get the runner. When he got the ball back, the fast-balling hurler let fly with another high hard one. And again Germany swung and missed. Disgustedly, he tossed away his bat and headed for the dugout.

"Hey, come back here," called the umpire. "You've only got two strikes."

"No, it's three strikes," growled Germany. "I also swung at that pitch he threw to first base!"

One of baseball's most famous clowns was a man named Al Schacht. Schacht was a failure as a big-league pitcher: in three seasons he won only ten games and lost fourteen. But as a clown he was superb.

One day when he was pitching for Jersey City in the minor leagues, his team led by one run when the skies darkened and it began to rain. Soon it was pouring. The field became a muddy swimming pool, but for some reason the umpire refused to call the game.

At the beginning of the next inning, Schacht trudged out to the mound carrying a pair of bats. He sat down in a puddle near the pitcher's mound and pretended to be rowing a boat, using the bats as oars. The umpire marched out to where Schacht sat.

"Al," he roared, "either start pitching or get out of the game!"

"I should get out, O'Brien," Schacht replied. "It's better than drowning."

"Start pitching or there'll be a big fine," warned the umpire.

Schacht got two men out, but then a batter got on base when his hit squished through the infield. The next batter swung viciously at one of Al's pitches and sent it over the fence for a home run. Now Jersey City was behind by a run. Just as Schacht got another ball to pitch, the umpire called the game and started walking off the field.

Disgusted, Al threw the ball high in the air. O'Brien, the umpire, saw the angry gesture and walked menacingly toward the mound. Just then, the ball came down—right on the umpire's head. Schacht ran all the way to the dressing room.

Leroy "Satchel" Paige was a colorful character who came into the majors late in life. Most of his career was spent in the Negro leagues before black

Satchel Paige in the uniform of the Kansas City Monarchs, then a leading team in the Negro leagues.

players were allowed to play in the majors. He came to the big leagues with a tremendous reputation as one of the great pitchers in the history of Negro baseball.

Satch played one game in Albany, Georgia, where the sheriff acted as umpire. Paige came to bat and hit a sharp line drive between the outfielders. By the time the ball was returned to the infield, Satch was standing on third. But the sheriff called him out for not touching second base.

Instead of starting an argument, Paige ran to second where the sheriff stood. He lay down on the ground and stuck his oversized feet almost into the sheriff's face.

"Look here, ump! How could I possibly miss second base with feet this big?" he said. The sheriff was furious and Satchel was dragged off the field feet first.

Satchel also had a few peculiar experiences in the Carribbean Islands, where baseball is almost a religion. The fans there take their baseball very seriously, and if a player makes a bonehead play, or strikes out with the bases loaded, he is likely to be greeted with a shower of fruits, vegetables and rotten eggs.

Paige was playing the outfield in one game. Just before the ball was pitched, he discovered a huge snake. A fly ball was hit his way, but he let the fly ball drop while he picked up a stick and beat the snake to death. Unfortunately the fly ball scored the winning run for the other team. Not only did the manager refuse to pay Satch for the game, but the fans chased him out of the ball park!

The national pastime has had a couple of players with huge appetites. One, "Shanty" Hogan, actually ate himself out of baseball. He was a huge man to begin with; in fact he was so large that he had to use a strap off a steamer trunk to hold up his pants.

Everybody pleaded with Shanty to quit eating so much, but he flatly refused. In desperation they tried to put him on a diet. If only he would pass up those rich desserts, the potatoes and the bowls of gravy, he might lose some weight. His manager, John McGraw, put him on a strict vegetarian diet and looked over all his restaurant bills before they were paid by the team.

Still, Shanty didn't lose weight. Instead he kept getting fatter day by day. The bills from the restaurant were for spinach, green peas, cooked carrots and other non-fattening foods. Why was Shanty still gaining weight?

The answer was really quite simple. Shanty had arranged a set of secret signals with the men in the kitchen. When he ordered green peas, they knew he meant bread and butter. Carrots were not carrots but chocolate layer cake. Spinach was the signal to send in another order of fried pork chops. McGraw was reading about vegetables, but Hogan was eating the whole menu.

Another hearty eater was an outfielder named Ping Bodie. Somehow, no matter how much Bodie ate, he never got too fat. One night somebody got the idea that it might be fun to have an eating contest between Bodie and an *ostrich*. Bodie accepted the challenge, but he insisted that there be only one item on the menu: spaghetti. Evidently the ostrich agreed, because that was what was served to the two contestants.

And Bodie won! He ate ten plates of spaghetti and Percy the ostrich also consumed ten. But as Bodie was hungrily reaching for plate number eleven, Percy's knees buckled and he passed out, ending the contest.

Perhaps the most famous eating incident in the big leagues concerned Babe Ruth. The Babe was the greatest home run hitter ever and the most famous and admired ballplayer of his time. But the whole country held its breath when Babe came down with the biggest bellyache in baseball history.

It must be explained first that Babe also had a tremendous appetite. His breakfast would consist of half a pound of bacon, four or five eggs, a dozen slices of toast, a few glasses of orange juice and about a quart of coffee. For dinner he might put away about a dozen ears of corn, some ham *and* chicken *and* beef, topped off with pie, cheese and ice cream.

And how that man loved hot dogs! One morning as the Yanks were going northward after spring training, Babe suddenly got hungry. He had had breakfast about eight o'clock, but now the train's dining car was closed. Babe knew he couldn't hold out until lunchtime. When the train stopped at Asheville, Babe hopped off and paid a fast visit to the station's hot dog stand, where he consumed twelve frankfurters and ten bottles of soda pop. He hopped back on the train.

Babe Ruth (left) with Yankee manager Miller Huggins.

Twenty minutes later he was rolling around on the floor of the train, holding his stomach, his face turning green. The train canceled its remaining stops and rushed straight through to New York without stopping. Babe was taken off the train on a stretcher and rushed to a hospital.

Anyone else would have learned a lesson. Not the Babe. As soon as the pain left, he began to complain to all his visitors. "They don't feed a guy enough to keep a bird alive," he moaned. "You know what I had for breakfast? *One* omelet! And they only used two eggs!"

Bill Veeck never played baseball, but he owned several major league teams at various times. The story of Veeck's midget pinch hitter is one of the great classics of baseball humor.

The idea of small people on big league teams wasn't very new. James Thurber once wrote a story about a midget who was a pinch hitter. It was called "You Could Look It Up". In the 1920s John McGraw had a dwarf who accompanied the Giants because McGraw thought he brought good luck. But Veeck was the only man who ever hired a midget to play for him.

Veeck owned the St. Louis Browns at that time, and the Brownies were a dreadful team. Few fans came to games, and Veeck was always trying to dream up new ways to draw crowds or at least attract some publicity for the team. Then he got his big idea.

Veeck went to Chicago, where he hired a midget named Eddie Gaedel. The deal called for Gaedel to play in only one game and have one turn at bat. Although Veeck kept it a secret that Gaedel was a midget, he officially notified the American League that he had hired a new player. No one had ever heard of Gaedel, but no questions were asked.

Getting a uniform for Gaedel was something of a problem. If Veeck had one made to order, someone might give away the secret. Fortunately St. Louis vice-president Bill DeWitt, Jr., had a seven-year-old son who had a Browns uniform. It fit the midget perfectly. Veeck decided that Gaedel's number should be 1/8 (one-eighth).

Then came the day of the big game. Gaedel was sneaked into the front office as though he were a spy on a secret mission. There Veeck gave him instructions.

"Now, all you have to do, Eddie, is go up to the plate with a toy bat and stand there. That's all. Just stand there. No matter what happens, *don't swing at the ball!*"

"O.K.," replied little Eddie. "But Mr. Veeck, I'm getting scared."

"There's nothing to be afraid of, Eddie," Veeck assured him. Then he added, "You're in show business. Just think of this as another appearance in a show. You'll become a mighty popular man."

Eddie was to appear in the second game of a doubleheader with the Tigers. Between the games there was a birthday party, and Eddie popped out of a huge cake as part of the celebration. The crowd thought it was very funny, but none of them knew what Veeck was planning. He let them know in the very first inning of the second contest.

When the Browns came to bat, the loudspeaker suddenly opened up. "Number one-eighth," called the announcer, "Eddie Gaedel now batting for Frank Saucier."

Out strode tiny Eddie Gaedel, carrying the toy bat on his shoulder.

Immediately the Detroit manager was out of the dugout to protest. The Brownie manager was ready. He ran up to the umpire, showing the papers from the American League front office which gave Eddie Gaedel the right to appear in the St. Louis lineup. There was nothing the umpire could do. Gaedel was entitled to take his turn at the plate.

Tiger pitcher Bob Cain stomped around at the mound, muttering to himself and kicking the resin bag savagely. Umpire Ed Hurley scratched his head sadly and sighed. Tiger catcher Bob Swift got down on his knees behind the plate.

Just to make matters worse for the pitcher, Eddie Gaedel took his stance in a crouch. There was no strike zone at all for him!

Cain didn't wind up. He lobbed the ball to his catcher as softly as he could. It sailed a foot over Gaedel's head.

"Ball one," intoned umpire Ed Hurley.

Again Bob Cain tossed the horsehide. "Ball two," said Hurley.

At the plate, midget Eddie Gaedel offered almost no strike zone for the pitcher to throw at.

By then the fans were hysterical. They stamped their feet, they clapped their hands, they laughed until the tears were streaming down their cheeks. The merriment finally got to pitcher Cain, then to the catcher and finally to the umpire. Soon they too were doubled over with laughter. Finally Cain calmed down enough to pitch, but he made no attempt to get a strike over the plate, realizing it was completely impossible. He just threw the ball. Gaedel never made a move to swing. And when ball four had sailed high and wide, he trotted down to first base. A pinch runner was sent in, and Gaedel took bows all the way back to the bench.

Gaedel disappeared from baseball for good, at least as a player. But years later when Veeck was owner of the Chicago White Sox, Gaedel and two other midgets landed on the playing field in a helicopter and emerged, dressed in space uniforms.

Using toy rocket guns they "captured" the Chicago second base combination of Fox and Aparicio. Later the ball players were released and presented with a scroll making them honorary Martians!

It's a well known fact that when a batter hits a fast ball, it will travel farther than if he had hit a slow pitch. Branch Rickey, who turned the St. Louis Cardinals into a great baseball powerhouse in the 1930s, believed the outfielders should know what their pitcher was throwing. If the pitcher was throwing a fast ball, they should play deeper. If it was going to be a slow pitch, they should play in closer.

"Heinie" Mueller, who played with the Cards, was instructed by Rickey to station himself according to the pitch called by the catcher.

"You'll know the signals," Rickey told the outfielder. "Now remember. Fast ball, play deep. Slow pitch, play closer."

The problem was that the fans also caught on to what Mueller was doing. When they saw him move back a few steps, the fans would chant, "Fast ball, Heinie. Back up." And when he moved in, they called out, "Slow pitch, Heinie. Move in."

One day Heinie walked in a few feet, and the batter knocked one way over his head for a triple. Actually the catcher had called for a fast ball, and when Mueller came back to the bench, Rickey took him to task.

"Didn't you see the signal for a fast one?" he demanded.

Heinie nodded. "Yeah, I saw it. But I just wanted to cross up those wise guys in the bleachers," he said resentfully. "They think they know everything."

A rookie named Kirk had an outstanding month in spring training. He knocked the ball a mile almost every time he came to bat. But once the season opened, he began to strike out regularly. He was good at hitting fast balls, but he couldn't hit a curve no matter how hard he tried. In a short time he found himself back in the minors.

One day he came to bat with men on first and third. The manager called a double steal. As the pitch came to the plate, the man on first headed for second, and the catcher threw to second. But the shortstop was ready for the double steal. He cut off the throw and fired the ball home to catch the runner who was coming from third. It was a beautiful throw—a perfect strike.

Kirk, who was still in the batter's box, took a vicious swing at the ball and hit a screaming line drive that reached the fence on one bounce. Of course he was declared automatically out for interfering with the play.

"Are you crazy?" demanded his manager. "Why did you swing at that return throw?"

"Because," said Kirk sullenly, "that was the

first straight ball I've seen in over a month, and I wanted to see if I could still hit!"

Today's ball players are good hitters, outstanding fielders, and the pitchers can throw hard. But somehow they are all very business-like. They don't get as much fun out of the game. Baseball is still a great game and an exciting game, but old-time fans keep wishing for another Rabbit Maranville, or a Rube Waddell, a Dizzy Dean or a Lefty Gomez. Not only were they great players, but also among the most colorful and amusing men in sports history!

INDEX

Page numbers in italics refer to photographs.

Alexander, Grover, 8
Altrock, Nick, 126
Ankenman, Fred, 77
Aparicio, Luis, 137
Atlanta, Ga., baseball team
    (minor league), 99
Averill, Earl, 57

Baker Field, Philadelphia,
    13
Barrow, Ed, 111, 113
Bartell, Dick, 66
Beck, Walter (Boom
    Boom), 13-14
Bellevue-Stratford Hotel,
    Philadelphia, 74-76
Birmingham, Ala., baseball
    team, 70
Bluege, Ossie, 55-56
Blues, Artie, 22
Bodie, Frank (Ping), 130-
    131
Boston Braves, 14-15, 18-20,
    21-28, 30-32, 87
Boston Red Sox, 60, 62, 64,
    115
Breadon, Sam, 93
Brooklyn Dodgers, 7-9, 12-
    14, *14*, 30, 59, 60, 67,

90-91, 96, 100-107, 108,
    120
Brucker, Earl, 71
Butler, Johnny, 101

Cain, Bob, 135-136
Carey, Andy, 15
Carey, Max, 12
Casore, Leon, 9-10
Chapman, Ben, 55
Chesbro, Jack, 113-114
Chicago Cubs, 29-30, 40,
    59-60, 94-95, 107, 123
Chicago White Sox, 69-70,
    124, 136
Cincinnati Reds, 65-66, 107
Cleveland Indians, 57, 65,
    123, 124
Cobb, Ty, 98
Cochrane, Mickey, 80
Collins, James (Rip), 95
Cooper, Wilbur, 29
Crosetti, Frank, 95, 115
Cuyler, Kiki, 99

Daley, Arthur, 15-16
Davis, Harry, 124
Dean, Jerome Herman
    (Dizzy), 74-95

early life, 76-77
Gas House Gang, 81-86
photographs of, *74, 75, 79, 89, 93*
Dean, Paul (Daffy), *74-75,* 76, 85-86, 89-92
DeBerry, Hank, 104
Delancey, Bill, 92
Derringer, Paul, 65-66, 107-108
Detroit, Mich., baseball team (minor league), 39
Detroit Tigers, 60, 64-66, 91-92, 98, 107, 123, 124, 134-136
DeWitt, Bill, Jr., 134
Dickey, Bill, 112, 118
DiMaggio, Dom, 87
DiMaggio, Joe, 15, 62, 87, 95, 120
DiMaggio, Vince, 87-88
Dowd, Tommy, 21
Dreyfuss, Barney, 29
Du Bois, Pa., baseball team, 37-38
Durocher, Leo, 81-83, *82,* 95

Edmonton, Canada, baseball team, 98
Elberfeld, Norman (Kid), 3-4
Evers, Johnny, 20

Feller, Bob, 43, 118
Fewster, Chick, 104-106

Finneran, Bill, 22
Fletcher, Art, 22
Ford, Whitey, 15
Fothergill, Bob, 81-82
Fournier, Jacques, 101
Fox, Nelson, 137
Foxx, Jimmy, 80, 117
Frisch, Frank, 81, 84, 90-91, 95

Gaedel, Eddie, 134-137, *136*
Gehrig, Lou, 121-122
Gehringer, Charlie, 91, 112
Geisel, Harry, 82
Gibson, George, 29
Gomez, Vernon (Lefty), 111-122
    as a hitter, 115
    as a pitcher, 117-120
    photographs of, *93, 110, 114, 119*
    superstitions, 113
Grand Rapids, Mich., baseball team, 39
Greenberg, Hank, 92
Greenville, N.C., baseball team, 59
Griffith, Clark, 60-61, 71
Grimm, Charlie, 28-29

Hall of Fame, 53
Hart, Bob, 22-23
Haynes, Joe, 69-70
Henrich, Tommy, 120
Herman, Floyd (Babe), 96-109
    as a baserunner, 102-106
    as a fielder, 102, 107

as a hitter, 106
early life, 98
photographs of, *97, 100, 103, 105*
Hoffman, Danny, 49
Hogan, James (Shanty), 129-130
Hollywood, Calif., baseball team, 107-108
Hornsby, Rogers, 101
Houston, Tex., baseball team, 77, 80,
Huggins, Miller, *132*
Hurley, Ed, 135

Jersey City, N.J., baseball team, 107, 126

Kankakee, Ill., baseball team, 6
Kansas City Blues baseball team, 5, 7
Kansas City, Mo., 5
Kansas City Monarchs baseball team, *128*
Kayhoe, Mike, 4
Kirk, 138-139
Klem, Bill, 11

Law, Ruth, 7
Lazzeri, Tony, 115
Leslie, Sam, 90
Little Rock, Ark., baseball team, 70
Louisville, Ky., baseball team (National League), 38, 40
Lucas, Arkansas, 76-77

Mack, Connie, 35, 41-50, *41*, 71, 78-80
Mantle, Mickey, 15
Maranville, Walter James Vincent (Rabbit), 18-33
career as manager, 30
early life, 21
major league career, 21-33
photographs of, *19, 24, 26, 31*
"vest-pocket catch," 27-28
Martin, John Leonard (Pepper), *75,* 76, 83-84, 86, 91, 95
Maysville, (Ky.), baseball team, 7
McCarthy, Joe, 115
McCormick, Frank, 66
McGraw, John, 10-12, 130, 133
McKechnie, Bill, 87
Medwick, Joseph (Ducky), 86, 95
Milan, Clyde, 123
Miller, Otto, 99
Milwaukee, Wis., baseball team (American League), 40
Minneapolis, Minn., baseball team, 51
Montgomery, Ala., baseball team, 3, 7
Mueller, Clarence (Heinie), 137-138

Nashville, Tenn., baseball team, 99

New Bedford, Mass., baseball team, 21

Newsom, Henry Louis (Bobo), 55-73
accidents, 55-58
early life, 58-59
major league career, 59-70
photographs of, *54, 64, 68, 72*
superstitions, 70-71

New York Giants, baseball team, 10-12, *11*, 18-20, 60, 133

New York Mets, 16-17

New York Yankees, 15-16, *16*, 55-56, 60, 64, 69-70, 111-122

Noren, Irv, 15

O'Doul, Lefty, 106

Omaha, Neb., baseball team, 98

Paige, Leroy (Satchel), 127-129, *128*

Pennock, Herb, 111

Phelps, Gordon, 12

Philadelphia Athletics, 35, 41-50, 60, 65, 67, 71, 78-80

Philadelphia Phillies, 10, 13-14

Pipgras, George, 111

Pittsburgh Pirates, 9-10, 28-29, 40, 77, 107

Punxsutawney, Pa., baseball team, 37-38, 41

Reardon, John (Beans), 82-83

Rickey, Branch, 76, 83-84, 137

Ripple, Jimmy, 66

Rizzuto, Phil, 120

Robinson, Wilbert, 7-8, 10, *100*, 100-104

Rodeo, California, 111

Rogers, Will, 33

Roosevelt, Franklin D., 55

Rowe, Lynwood (Schoolboy), *64*, 91

Ruffing, Red, 111

Ruth, Babe, 116, 131-133, *132*

St. Joseph, Mo., baseball team, 77

St. Louis Browns, 43-44, 50, 60, 61, 63-64, 67, 133

St. Louis Cardinals baseball team, 30-32, 76-94

Saucier, Frank, 135

Schacht, Al, 126

Schaefer, Herman (Germany), 123-126

Scheetz, 6

Schmidt, Butch, 21

Scott, Jack, 25

Schreckengost, Ossie, 47

Seattle, Wash., baseball team, 100, 108

Shanks, Hank, 125-126
Shelbyville, Ky., baseball team, 6
Simmons, Al, 80
Springfield, Mass., 21
Spuhler, Henry, 37-38
Stallings, George, 22
Stengel, Charles Dillon (Casey), 1-17
  as coach and manager, 12-17
  early life, 5-6
  major league career as player, 7-12
  photographs of, *2, 11, 14, 16*
  sparrow incident, 9-10
Stengel, Grant, 5
Street, Gabby, 7, 77-80
Swift, Bob, 135
Syracuse, N.Y., baseball team, 107

Terry, Bill, 84, 106
Thorpe, Jim, 18-20
Thurber, James, 133
Tierney, Jim, 28-29
Toledo, Ohio, baseball team, 51-52, 107

Van Atta, Russ, 32

Vance, Dazzy, 104-106
Veeck, Bill, 133-137

Waddell, George Edward (Rube), 35-53
  disappearances, 39, 44, 50-51
  early life, 36-39
  election to Hall of Fame, 53
  minor league career, 39-40
  photographs of, *34, 46, 52*
Wagner, Honus, 22, 28
Washington Monument, 7
Washington Senators, 55-56, 60, 67, 71, 121, 123
Weaver, Hal, 59
Whaling, Moose, 21
Whitehead, Burgess, 88
Wilson, Hack, 13
Wright, Glen, 29
Wrigley, Phil, 94-95

Yankee Stadium, N.Y., 113
Yellowhorse, Moses, 28-29
Yingling, Earl, 51-52
York, Rudy, 69-70

Zimmerman, Heinie, 20-21